TIME
CHORDS

~ STONES
~ DROWNING

A Memoir

PETER SIMON KARP

Copyright © 2012 by Peter Simon Karp.

Library of Congress Control Number: 2012910008
ISBN: Hardcover   978-1-4771-2337-9
              Softcover   978-1-4771-2336-2
              Ebook   978-1-4771-2338-6

While the core events in this memoir are true, this is a work of fiction. Names, characters, places and dialogues are the product of the author's imagination or are composites drawn from different sources and different times and are used fictitiously.

This book was printed in the United States of America.

To order additional copies of this book, contact:
Xlibris Corporation
1-888-795-4274
www.Xlibris.com
Orders@Xlibris.com
94392

TIME
CHORDS

~ STONES
~ DROWNING

For Mona Pecheux Karp

The core events in these stories are true, seen from the interior of a young boy's mind and flashed back through the dark lens of an old man's remembrances.

Memory is captured, contained in time chords, some of which soar and inspire our spirit, while others may dwarf us and claw at our beings for a lifetime.

TIME CHORDS

STONES

Dark cumulus clouds cross overhead. In the distance, the boy hears a mechanical roaring sound. The skies are fast becoming a whirling mass of dark energy. Inside leather work boots, his naked toes feel the earth begin to quiver. Aloft, suspended in flight, he watches a young boy chug his way up a steep, treelined country road passing the rock-wall property line of his grandfather's small farm. Hidden behind the nineteenth-century farmhouse is his home: a wood-framed white bungalow that his father and grandfather built with their own hands seven summers ago. Sensing dark motion, physical danger approaching, the boy tries to force his heavy work boots to accelerate homeward, but he is unable to move any faster than at a snail's pace, barely progressing.

Frustrated, his mind's eye dives back to earth and he is transformed: no longer a spectator, he is locked inside the chubby boy's body, feeling strong vibrations underfoot as waves ripple down the macadam roadway. The distant mechanical roaring seems closer, multiplying by the second as if in sync with the metronomic clicking of his schoolhouse clock. Confused by these night thoughts, the boy's vision miraculously curls over the far side of the hilltop and he comes upon a frightening sight: a rolling out of black-and-white newsreel images as the German army division prepares to advance down the roadway—Nazi motorcycles with sidecars, followed by a fleet of *armored trucks that look like cattle cars and are filled with hordes of black-helmeted Nazi storm troopers. Overwhelmed by these battlefield images, the boy pinches his cheek but feels no physical reaction. When did the war start? When was their peaceful farm community invaded by these frightening Blackshirts? No, he couldn't have slept through it. But right now, under a blitzkrieg attack, it may be too late for him to escape!*

Images of war flow out of the darkness, all very dense and cluttered, yet each action seems painfully real. In the morning darkness, he watches German armored trucks roar over the hilltop led by a dozen Nazi motorcycle assassins. He must stop watching and take action if he hopes to escape but bodily movement abandons him. Caught in the energy field of their bright oncoming headlights, it is instantly clear that he must hurl his body off the macadam road and throw himself over the rock wall. Inside those rocks, families of black snakes may be hiding. No matter. He must dive headfirst past them and roll his young body into the safety of the high brown grass under the grove of fir trees. He must move instantly if he hopes to survive; what can be stopping him?

Rising high above the impending collision of forces, he sees the problem: the chubby boy's boots seem stuck in the macadam which has boiled over and hardened into cement. It is impossible to lift his feet! Hundreds of earthworms appear and surround him, crawling across the road as if the aftermath of a heavy summer rain. Diving down into the struggling boy's body once more, he screams out in desperation, trying to will his mind to take command of the boy's motor functions, but he seems powerless. The roaring sound of advancing Nazi forces becomes louder, rocketing through his inner ears. The boy lifts his head bravely to face the oncoming blitz just as Nazi motorcycles emerge from the swirling fog, their engines coughing noxious black smoke as they accelerate. Gods of destruction are on the loose, and he's fixed in their path, about to become a sacrificial lamb. The boy opens his mouth to scream "Stop!" But he can't hear the sound of his own voice beneath the overwhelming tumult of the black-shirted Nazi motorcyclists riding side by side and bearing down on him, engines spewing out that evil-smelling black smoke. Only his mind seems capable of flight; the rest is trapped inside the boy's helpless body. Motor sounds of the highest register imaginable rage through his brain, shredding any hope of escape. As the helmeted riders roar down at him with every ounce of bloodthirsty Nazi primal force, he is miraculously able to see their fierce eyes locked beneath dark goggles and see the hatred foam over on their thin lips and savage, deeply lined faces. His eyes tightly shut, he listens for that life-destroying moment—the crash of fiery steel and huge rubber tires into the soft midsection of his own flesh. The boy holds his breath and waits for his shriek of certain death!

Instantly, his nightmare ends. Or does it? Did he awaken in time or has the boy been smashed to bits? The horror of the Nazi cyclists' hillside blitzkrieg is palpable. He can still taste their smoke and noxious gasoline, unable to rid his stomach of nausea. While safe in bed, it is naive to think they no longer exist because he's awakened. No, real Nazis exist outside his dark window, elsewhere at the moment, swooping down winding European roads, overwhelming cities, towns and villages, and capturing innocent people. Ruthless killers, out to annihilate them all, and destroy him too; as a Jew, he is among their targeted. Storm troopers he's never met or dared challenge are obsessed with ridding the world of a race of people like him. How obsessed are they? Crazed enough to pick up a Jewish baby from its stroller, swing it by one leg, and slam its screaming head against the corner of a concrete building, dashing its brains out! This tale of horror beyond belief he overheard from an old Jewish lady in a shawl whispering to her friend—a secret to be hidden from all but the very brave.

His new friend, Peter, a twelve-year-old refugee four years his senior, had firsthand experience before escaping from Germany. The boys play together once or twice a month, and he tells Joseph all about the "war-crazy Nazis bastards" who believe it's their destiny to conquer the Western world, rid it of all Jews and Gypsies, and create a new race of blond, blue-eyed Aryans. A rumble of wings flutters through the morning darkness. He shudders, catching his breath; it's hard to breathe when the air is dense with such evil, unthinkable aspirations. The boy drifts back into a half sleep, entering a netherworld where future shadow images of war with Germany wrestle in the darkness. Joseph's mind dwells on savage, deeply lined Nazi faces smelling of gas fumes and gunpowder—out to blow up homes, shoot unarmed boys and girls his own age and leave their naked, mangled bodies to die in muddy streets. Deeply lined German faces that never blink or shed a drop of human compassion.

Black-and-white newsreels play silently across his white stucco ceiling. Aircraft batteries explode noiseless firecrackers into space and bundles of dark energy cascade down, encircling his bedside. Half-asleep, Joseph seeks a safe place within his mind to hide; he prays that the Satan who's invaded his night thoughts will be sufficiently pleased by the fear inflicted to simply roar out in brutal laughter and fade away. And it's done. As suddenly as they began, the fireworks exhibition ends. The last sparks drift downward, sinking into the hardwood cracks and crevices of his bedroom floor where they magically disappear. All is gone now, the dark energy transformed into solid, benign, everyday mass.

Flushed with sweat and shaken by the vividness of his nightmare, Joseph shrinks down in his bed and tucks his head under the wool blanket. These nightmare images, he knows, stem from cinema newsreels or from Grandfather's newspapers. Most afternoons, the two sit together and watch jet-black ink overrun the map of Europe in Grandfather's *World Telegram & Sun*. Black arrows with swastikas inside marked the Nazi blitzkrieg across Poland a year ago and now motors across Holland and Belgium, cutting past France's unbreakable Maginot Line defense to encircle Paris and triumph—an unthinkably fast surrender by a proud French army. They watch frightening black-ink swastika arrows pursue the British armies to the edge of the English Channel, but the British escape from Dunkirk one miraculous week when flotillas of little ships—fishing boats, cruisers and sailboats—sneak across the Channel and rescue 340,000 British soldiers to fight another day. Now a Nazi bombing blitz begins to strike London and other English cities night after night, bombing civilians to soften the British will to fight while the German army mobilizes its forces, threatening to invade. The boy and his grandfather share common fears that jet-black swastika arrows will soon flutter their wings over the Channel and spread their destructive black ink across all of England, Scotland, Wales, and a neutral Ireland. America could be next, unless President Roosevelt capitulates to the Bundsmen's wishes and signs a phony peace treaty with Hitler, who, Peter insists, "we must never, never trust!" It will be difficult for Germany to invade America with the great Atlantic Ocean between us. "The Nazis will lure us over to fight alongside England," Peter boldly predicts, "then attack us on the soil of Europe. I fear that no country, not even America, can stop the incredible war machine Hitler has created." Joseph listens to Gabriel Heatter's deeply troubled baritone voice on Grandfather's crystal set; night after night, this troubadour of dark realities pauses a dramatic moment and begins his nightly broadcasts stating, "There's bad news tonight!"

Pitch-black outside, still deep into night, but the boy is afraid to risk falling asleep and sliding back into his Nazi nightmare. He lifts his head out from under the heavy woolen blanket and listens intently, trying to read the sounds of the road outside his window. Most mornings at daybreak, he listens for groups of out-of-work men walking the country roads in search of a job or just a few hours work or asking, not begging, for food. A great Depression is nearly over, and fewer men and women now walk the roads. "Franklin Delano Roosevelt has cut off the head of the Depression snake," Grandfather reads aloud. But desperate men still raid their chicken coops after dark to steal eggs or make off with hens. Shrieks from kidnapped chickens as loud as any siren cause Grandfather to jump into his overalls and load his shotgun then make his way to the chicken coops out back with his nasty little spitz to protect his flock. The thieves know he never fires to hurt them, but he shoots straight up into the air to scare them off. So they grab their stolen loot, twist the necks of the shrieking hens, and their shadowy figures disappear deep into the backwoods' thickets, where they know the old man will never dare chase after them.

German Bundsmen are much more dangerous. A year ago just after sundown, the boy sat on the staircase inside the farmhouse's front door behind his tense grandfather, who was hunched forward with his shotgun loaded. They'd turned out all the lights and waited for the small, frightening gang of German-American Bundsmen to march up the road toward the Davies Hill campsite carrying both American and German flags and then breaking into song with their loud, guttural voices. While most Bundsmen drove cars to the site, Grandfather had been warned about marchers by Cropsey, a good German who rents some of his fields in summer to plant corn and beans. As a precaution, Joseph's parents took the baby away to Bubby Sarah's house, but the boy wanted to stay with his grandfather. As the only Jews living along that stretch of country road between the village and the campsite, there was no telling what the wild gang of Bundsmen might do when they marched past the farmhouse. Joseph listened so intently that he kept hearing small acorns hit the roof of their side porch. The chanting Bundsmen halted directly in front of the farmhouse and they became extraordinarily silent. *Will they smash our mailbox or throw stones at our greenhouse's glass windows, or worse?* Joseph fears the worst: that they might decide to break America's laws and force their way into Grandfather's farmhouse? The boy holds his breath, hoping the Bundsmen can't see their faces hidden behind the curtained glass on their front door.

Outside, he hears Bundsmen whispering, their shadows huddled close together, deciding what action to take. It was too quiet, too frighteningly still. Joseph can hear their lowered voices conspiring. He knows that Grandfather won't kill a mosquito if he can avoid it, but watching the old man load and cock his shotgun, the boy senses that his peace-loving grandfather is about to break his life's precious commandment. It won't be a question of shooting another human but of lawful protection of his own family and property. "A man's home is his castle," the law says. And yet, Joseph wonders whether neighbors will call the police if they hear shots fired. Will the village police come quickly or take their time? Hard to tell who will be their friends, or who'll be frightened into becoming their enemies by passive default. "Bystanders always make the difference in a time of crisis," old gaptooth Thomas lectured him afterward. A few tense minutes pass. Then, a loud crashing sound, metal against metal, as a hammer or crowbar smashes down, destroying their mailbox. Joseph swallows his own saliva, watching the shadows and listening for the sound of their next aggressive act. There is a moment of sudden anguish when a large Bundsman leaps up onto the front lawn, trying to incite a reaction from those inside the farmhouse. The earth stands still for

Joseph as he watches the large man's dark shadow dance toward them. Then, a shrill command. Their voices become louder, more like normal voices, as the Bundsmen decide to move on, thank the Lord! He listens to the echoes of their scary marching song fading into the distance as Bundsmen snake their way up the road toward their overnight meeting ground to join nearly a hundred fellow Fascists in burning Christian crosses and planning their next aggressive action to keep America out of war with Germany.

Joseph watches the tension leave the back of Grandfather's sweat-covered neck and shoulders as the old man rises and carefully places his shotgun on its hallway rack. Well, bless be God, they'd been untouched physically. But it wasn't over yet. The same mob of Bundsmen is expected to return next morning after their night of fiery speeches, cross burnings, and drinking hard country applejack. Except it never happened, thank the Lord. Instead, a convoy of cars and trucks came to pick the Bundsmen up at the campsite early next morning, and they drove past the farm shouting undecipherable curses from their open car windows. Joseph is depressed to realize that so many Nazi sympathizers live close around them. They'd held a massive rally in Madison Square Garden in New York City, his grandfather told him, which led to fighting in the city streets. From now on, he thinks it will be hard to tell who are our friends and who are enemies. Who can we trust anymore?

"The Führer has German sympathizers lined up along the streets to welcome his troops in every country he conquers," Peter says, "France included, and it looks like he has much too many Nazi lovers among the Germans over here, too." Maybe Hitler doesn't need a massive invasion of America after all. Maybe if he ships a few well-armed divisions of his powerful army across the Atlantic, tens of thousands of Bundsmen and Nazi sympathizers will rise up to join them in a battle for America. The thought of thousands of Nazi sympathizers rising up to fight for the future of America was truly disturbing to the young boy, setting off his original Nazi troop-invasion nightmares.

Joseph's blitzkrieg nightmare took place on the same country road on which the real-life Bundsmen marched. The black cloud that the Nazi motorcyclists emerged from evoked the same horror and fears of victimization that the boy felt while sitting in total darkness on the staircase behind his grandfather. The old man's hands were trembling on his shotgun's trigger while the boy silently prayed that the Bundsmen won't launch an anti-Semitic attack to show the power of their movement and to glorify their Aryan superiority. For several minutes afterward, Grandfather leaned back on the staircase, shook his head sadly, and ran his fingers through his thick white hair. Then he became his old upbeat self again, worried about everything and nearly everyone, but with a pleasant, bemused disposition. Only mobs of Nazi Bundsmen could shake him from the positive karma he feels about almost everyone he meets in what he teaches Joseph is "this extraordinary country and miraculous planet." Even desperate men who steal his chickens and eggs, the major source of his family's livelihood, cannot make him hate them. So how can anyone, the boy wonders, even bloodthirsty Nazi Bundsmen, hate a man as honest, good, and gentle as his grandfather just because he happened to be born a Jew?

Germans are men too, but they are "a race devoted to bloody wars of conquest over the ages," his grandfather's newspapers proclaim. And now, led by a wild-eyed Hitler, their self-proclaimed dictator with a desire to rule the world, they'd turned into a crazed mob whose mission is to strike quickly, blitzkrieg their enemies while they are weak, afraid, and helpless, then seize their cities and countries one by one. He learned all about them from Peter, who'd escaped from Berlin two years before with his parents, both doctors and research scientists. On their monthly playdates, the older boy can't stop explaining to young Joseph what the Nazis do to you if you are a Jew, how hate is cultivated by all their leaders and spread like weeds, especially among the fierce Hitler youth. Peter was made to wear a Star of David whenever he dared go out into the Berlin streets, his parents were fired from their hospital jobs even though they converted to Christianity, and Peter was thrown out of school, which he didn't mind so much because of Nazi youth taunts and threats of beatings. He didn't mind being home alone, safe and cozy next to a warm brick fireplace in the library with all of his family's "unlawful books" to read. "But they don't leave you alone even at home." Peter tells Joseph how Nazis started rounding up any Jew they didn't like or any who looked at them in a scared or funny way or anyone some rotten spy said is a troublemaker, and they send them off to work camps along with Communists and other enemies of the state. How everyone starves in work camps.They force you to do physical labor every day from dawn to dusk no matter what the weather. Diseases, like typhus, spread, and it's tough for the old or weak to survive. "No way a Jew can escape them with the policemen and all the judges on their side," Peter explains. "And you're a Jew, Hitler decreed, if one of your grandparents has a single drop of Jewish blood. So it didn't matter that we converted to Christianity. Worst of all," Peter said, his high voice choking, "was to see so many old friends of my parents, who we thought were good Germans, turn on us and accept the Aryan maniacs and Herr Hitler's Fascist government. They all bought into Hitler's master-race politics—even our friends, our servants and my father's professional colleagues. None of them wanted to be left out. It's a powerful idea to most Germans. They're on a holy mission to conquer the world and purify it. All it takes to create their new world order is *willpower*. They have the willpower to make our worst fears come true, unless America joins with Mr. Churchill and builds better tanks, planes and weapons to stop them. But I wonder whether anyone has the willpower to stop them." The older boy pulls out his soiled handkerchief and, looking distraught, wipes the sweat pouring down his pale, white face.

"Why do they hate Jews so much?" Joseph asks, and Peter breaks out laughing as if confronted by the worst kind of naive fool. "Jews are always the scapegoats. Read your history. Jews crucified Jesus. Haven't the Christian kids told you what Jews and Romans did two thousand years ago? In Germany, Hitler calls Jews the cowards who surrendered our country in the Great War. It's the Jews, he screams, who sold out our brave German soldiers and signed the Treaty of Versailles, bankrupting our country. It's Jews, he screams, who caused the worldwide Depression, who betrayed us, promised to keep Germany small and poor and weaponless, and who promised to pay millions to the French and English. Our brave German soldiers never lost the War, Hitler screams, it's the Jews and Weimar Socialists who betrayed us. Who decides what is true? Herr Hitler does. He decides Nazis are the true Aryan master race created to conquer the world and rule it. Supermen! Super-duper supermen! That's Germany's destiny as long as its Aryan blood is kept pure and not diseased by the inferior blood of Jews, Socialists, or Gypsies. He screams it out at the top of his lungs, and all but a handful of German resisters believe in him. He's got the whole nation hypnotized, like my father says. Nazi youth are in the streets ready to do anything to us Juden to prove their loyalty to der Füher's cause and grow up to become noble SS officers!" All strength seems to drain from Peter after this outburst. His cheeks redden, and his thin, ascetic body sinks down into the mud and weed-filled grass on the outskirts of their make-believe cattle ranch.

Peter refuses to play war games. He loves American cowboys and Indians of the old West, loves being a farmer or rancher with his toy horses, sheep, cows, dogs, and miniature cowhands. While years older, he and Joseph play in the mud for hours, suspending time as they build lakes, rivers, and mountains to expand their *Lone Star* ranch's acreage and herds across the great western states of Wyoming and Montana. Rarely did Peter's underground humor show itself: like the day he broke out in his bittersweet resistance song,*"Ven der Führer says ve ist der master race, ve heil, heil right in der Füher's face / for to love der Führer is a great disgrace / so ve heil, heil* [farting sounds, he laughs] *right in der Füher's face!"* Peter is really smart, close to brilliant, but he isn't very strong. He's a diabetic who needs to take shots of insulin several times a day just to stay alive. He was lucky to escape from Germany, Joseph thinks. The Nazis would have sent him off to a work camp where it wasn't likely that he'd survive a week under their cruel guards. Joseph wonders whether he'd have the courage and strength to survive if the Nazis invaded America, a horror he truly fears, which is why his Nazi nightmares frighten him, carrying their cruel stream of violence over from the brightness of day. Will he, like the chubby boy in his nightmare, panic and freeze and let the Nazi monsters roll over him, turn him into another powerless victim of Hitler's storm troopers with their lack of human feeling toward any boy born a Jew? That's why it's so important to try to grow up faster, to learn to defend himself and to train really hard so he will never give in and let the Hitler youth bully him too.

"Hey! What? What're you doing?" Joseph wakes to a jolt of cold water splashed across his face and shoulders and onto the bedsheets.

"Time to wake up!" Joseph's father is splashing him with extracold water taken from the well, a last resort when trying to wake the boy from one of his "deep-Indian sleeps," as gaptooth Thomas calls them. "While lasting for hours, it feels like seconds since your head touched the pillow, and you wake up tired and aching as if you hadn't slept at all." Old Thomas, a devout Christian, lives out back in a chicken coop over summer months and helps Grandfather on the farm; come fall, he works his way across the country to Arizona or New Mexico. Thomas insists that Indians he lived with on their native reservations out West always complained about being tired and aching, not at all like the wild, colorful braves who had to be shot twice from their horses but kept bouncing back every week to appear in next Saturday's cowboy cinema. Must be all the wild and crazy young Indian braves got killed in those gun battles to win the West, the boy concluded, and only the tired and sleepy ones survive today.

"Hurry up! You can't afford to be late to school again, and have that teacher send notes home," Father yells. "Get going. Wash up and eat. I'll drive you as soon as you're ready."

Joseph is shivering from the blast of cold water and confused, trying to get his bearings. Today is Monday He last had school on Friday. It's the beginning of October. Chilly out. He'll need a jacket. Something else keeps gnawing at him. Why can't he remember? The boy senses a terrible threat hanging over him on Monday in school, but he can't remember what trouble is in store for him or why. No matter. Whatever, it can't be half so bad as his Nazi nightmares or Bundsmen marching past to burn their crosses. He grabs his rumpled clothes and runs naked into the warm bathroom to wash and dress. Can it be homework? No, he is pretty sure he's done it all. More likely, there was none. School is pretty easy in the early grades. Joseph gulps down a bowl of Wheaties cereal with milk and a lot of sugar; he doesn't have time to make a peanut butter sandwich for lunch, so he plucks a banana from the stalk and an apple from the bowl and stuffs them into a brown paper bag. Getting to school on time is a real problem for someone who has deep-Indian sleeps two or three times a week. Mother has trouble getting up in the morning too, but that's because she reads her novels late into the night and she can't put them down until she finishes and learns who dies in the end, who marries who, or who becomes a saint and sets a great example for us all. When he was younger, Joseph would run into her bedroom to give Mother a kiss before leaving for school, but he is nearly eight years old—too big for that now. Besides, she'd just roll over, eyes closed, and mumble, "Don't wake me, I was up half the night feeding the baby." Everything is different since his baby sister was born early that summer. His mother has no time left to teach him or read books like Don Quixote fencing with his windmills, and laugh aloud together, little time to pay much attention to him at all.

"Holy jeezus!" Joseph yells, seeing the clock in the hall as he wipes his mouth and races out to his father's waiting car. The school warning bell is about to ring, and his classmates are already inside hanging their coats up and taking their seats. "Shit," he whispers as he slams the car door, "no way I can get there on time." Father makes a growling sound. *Shit* may be one of Father's favorite words, but he hates to hear it from Joseph's lips. Father growls again, guns his rebuilt Studebaker's engine, and swings the car out onto the steep country road heading down toward the village, the county courthouse, and the elementary school. Joseph looks out the back window up the road where Nazi motorcyclists with sidecars emerged from a cloud and roared down toward his helplessly stuck body. No sign of them now. Not a Nazi vehicle in sight. America's war with Germany has remained in his dreams. Joseph smiles to himself. Reality is so much better than his nightmares. Then the boy remembers the terrible threat that hangs over him in school today, and he breaks out into a sweat.

How stupid could he be? Why hadn't he remembered? Old maid Ms. Cunningham, his teacher, had worked up intense anger toward Joseph for being late on Friday and threatened that if he was late to school one more time, she'd make all of her homeroom classes stay after school with him as punishment. Having this deep-Indian sleep problem and his mother up half the night feeding their new baby, Joseph has the worst lateness record by far in all her classes. It infuriates Ms. Cunningham to a breaking point whenever he shows up late and tries to sneak into his seat. But why would she want to punish all his classmates for his lateness? he wonders. Why not send a note home or call for a conference with his parents? Maybe she knows there's a new baby and doesn't want to bother his mother?

No, it's her meanness coming out. She's determined to get even with me, Joseph knows. She said she won't tolerate his stubborn disobedience one more time. From the beginning, she never liked him, believed that his lateness was an act meant to spite or defy her. So she made the nastiest threat she could think of, one that didn't even make sense to him at first. While frightened, Joseph feels pretty sure she'll never carry out her threat even if she remembers it. Most times, it's far better to be absent. Joseph is absent a lot too, but absences seem much less of a problem for old Ms. Cunningham personally than actually watching Joseph's trembling young body stumble through the door late and disturb her classes. By the time Father's car pulls into the gravel driveway and empty playground in front of the boxlike two-story wooden schoolhouse, Joseph has worked himself into a state of deep panic. It would be better if he was sick, if he went back home and didn't cause an interruption for the teacher or his classmates. So he tells Father that he feels a real bad stomachache coming on. But Father will have none of it.

"Get out! You'll feel better when you open your books and your mind starts working." Father nudges him out, pulls the Studebaker door shut and drives off quickly, leaving Joseph alone on the deserted playground to face the anger of Ms. Cunningham and all of his homeroom classmates if she keeps her vow. *Why didn't Father understand? Why can't I talk to him? He never wants to listen, so we never really talk to each other.* Anyway, the boy feels too ashamed of himself and his own inadequacies to try to explain the teacher's threats of punishment to his parents. *All they worry about anyway is my report card and how well I do on tests.* While he usually did pretty well in school, it never seemed good enough for them. He knows that he'll never live up to his father's academic success or be the winner of the only county scholarship to college.

Father's car has driven completely out of sight. Joseph pauses now, entertains the idea of sneaking off and playing truant for the day. He enjoys walking the back roads and exploring new pathways through the woods. A few hours of pleasurable trekking then he can show up distressed and tell his mother he was sent home sick. Mother is always at her Russian best, warm and very caring, whenever he is sick, so Joseph has a good feeling about going home to Mother, being put to bed, and being given some great-tasting food or dessert to make him feel better. To trek home through the backwoods is sure to be a grand adventure, and to show up home around noon is an excellent plan.

At that moment, Joseph catches sight of the janitor's stern face peering out of a tiny basement window watching his every move. Being a small-town elementary school, Wendell the janitor doubles as truant officer. No way out now with Wendell the janitor watching. Joseph feels boxed in, a helpless target much like the boy in his dream. But when things get tough, he remembers old gaptooth Thomas lecturing him, "A man's got to shut off his mind and take one small step after another until he finds he's walked on past his troubles. No one ever said life would be easy." Joseph takes one last look at the downstairs window and sees Wendell gesturing him inside. Reluctantly, he walks up the steps and swings open the heavy schoolhouse front door. High on the wall facing the doorway, the big hand of the oversized school clock loudly clicks off another minute late. No way to turn the clock back. He is showing up for school nearly twenty-three minutes late, his worst lateness ever! *How can I go in there and face her?*

The hallway is empty, but he hears classes in session, teachers' voices and sudden laughter from pretty Mrs. Koch's lively third and fourth grade classroom. In total, there are four teachers who double up to cover elementary grades K-thru-12. Ms. Cunningham teaches three classes—kindergarten, first and second grades. Joseph started school at an early age and is now in second grade. All his school years he's had only one teacher—pink-cheeked, plump old Ms. Cunningham who took an instant dislike of him from the first day of school. He tried to ignore it, but big loudmouth Natalie told Joseph that the teacher said, of all her kids, there's only one she truly dislikes. "If she meant you," Mother explained, "you'd best look into your own actions and attitudes toward her that are causing the problem. No, I'm sure it has nothing to do with that nonsense about you being different or being the only Jewish student in the school and out for the holidays." That was before Mother actually met her. Joseph stands frozen outside her classroom door, wondering how long he can stand out there and not be noticed. He tries to remember when his problem with Ms. Cunningham began. Mother taught him to read well before he started kindergarten. With three classes in one room, Joseph couldn't help but start to lip-read along with the first and second graders, mouthing the words silently at first then whispering a little louder in a pleasant, self-satisfied way, especially when one of the older kids paused too long or stumbled over words that came so easily to Joseph. Ms. Cunningham noticed him reading along during that first week of school. In what was a totally surprising reaction, the plump, red-cheeked teacher became furious at Joseph; she grabbed a favorite wooden ruler off her desk and smacked him on his wrists, knocking the textbook to the floor and splitting its binding. She started to breathe very loudly, and the veins on her neck expanded. The teacher growled out that she won't tolerate what she called his total disobedience of her rules, and she repeated that several times to make sure he understood her. Joseph sat there humiliated and stunned. From then on, she was a bulldog, growling at his every move. And whenever she found him hiding storybooks under his desk to lip-read along with the first or second graders, she'd slap out at him with her yardstick, take the book away and several times make him sit in the dunce corner for a whole period. Unable to break him of this habitual urge to read along "to show off how smart he was," she sent a note home saying she wanted to meet with his parents. They didn't know the reason, and Joseph wasn't able to help them understand what might be wrong.

The teacher began the meeting by confronting them in a most genteel manner. Didn't they agree that their son, Joseph, had a most worrisome attitude showing off to his older classmates by lip-reading aloud and not doing the crayon coloring or drawings in the workbook that she'd assigned to his kindergarten section? Father mentioned he'd been skipped ahead a class or two at Joseph's age for perhaps some of these same reasons. "Well, our school doesn't skip children," Ms. Cunningham chided him. "We believe character is the single most important lesson we can teach our students in their early school years. We have no patience with children who think they are too smart or too good to listen and learn to obey their teachers. With three classes to teach in my one little homeroom, I have no time for any smart—" "Smart ass!" Mother later filled in the blanks. Normally Joseph's father, with his advanced college degrees, would have challenged her remarks intellectually or put her down with a show of detached wit, but he immediately recognized the bulldog they were up against, seeing that it was her turf and she'd emerge a sure winner. So Father nodded and caved, which wasn't like him at all. Emboldened, Ms. Cunningham informed them that she favored a thick wooden ruler, and she used it in her strong right hand whenever a child was out of line, a practice she'd learned in Catholic school from the rigorous Nuns who taught her. If any parents have objections to her methods, they can take it up with the Principal. Their meeting ended in a forced silence between people quite uncomfortable with one another; Joseph's parents departed quickly with what seemed like cordial but muted goodbyes.

"Well, what are you waiting for?" shouts the large, bass-voiced janitor, Wendell, who'd sneaked up behind him. Trapped, Joseph strips off his jacket and opens the classroom door and, trying to be quiet as an Indian in a leafy forest, he tiptoes toward his seat in the back row. It was a wonderful silent moment, as if in slow motion. Ms. Cunningham, head down, hunched over her desk, is listening as the first graders read aloud, and she doesn't seem to notice his entrance.

"Joseph's here!" big Natalie shouts out to get everyone's attention. "He's trying to sneak into his seat!" The teacher looks up, glaring out at her. "If you have something to say, young lady, raise your hand and wait until I call on you." Big Natalie sinks down in her desk, not daring to say anything more. Ms. Cunningham rises, ruler in hand, and walks slowly toward Joseph's desk in the back row of the classroom.

"Did you really think you could sneak into class so late that I wouldn't notice you?" "No, Ma'am," he mumbles, stammering. "What did you say?"

Joseph tries to clear his throat. "I said no, Ma'am, I didn't want to bother anyone."

Ms. Cunningham straightens her back until she towers over the seated boy, and she becomes increasingly intense, smacking the yardstick into the palm of her thick left hand. "I've had enough of you and your continual lateness interrupting all three of my classes! I told you last Friday would be the last time I would tolerate your lateness!" "Sorry, Ma'am. I'll never be late again, I swear it."

"Did you tell your mother what I'd do if you were late one more time?"

"No, Ma'am, I forgot to tell her."

"Well, what is your excuse this time? Why didn't your mother get you up in time?"

"She had morning sickness," he stammers, trying to explain. "She was up all night with the baby's infection."

The class breaks out in laughter, but the old maid teacher doesn't think it is either funny or a respectable excuse; she glares across the classroom, and the children become very silent. "Can't take proper care of one child and they have another," she mutters accusingly. "Well, I'm not going to waste my good ruler on you this time. But I promise you, you'll never be late for my class ever again. Never!" And the furious teacher turns away, returning to her cluttered desk in front of the classroom.

The teacher hadn't spoken about her threat to punish them all. Did she forget? For a moment, the boy feels relieved, picturing himself as a prisoner on murderers' death row about to be unfairly executed, but at the last minute receiving a pardon from an honorable, fair-minded Governor with wavy gray hair, a firm jaw, and a smile you can trust. Maybe Thomas is right: "Hold your chin up and take a first step, then a second, and you may find you've walked right on past the trouble you feared most." Maybe it's true, Joseph thinks, holding back a smile; maybe she puts the blame on Mother. Didn't she say, some women shouldn't have children. That very instant, Ms. Cunningham rises to address the class in one of her most foul moods, announcing,

"Attention! You all heard me warn Joseph last Friday that our entire homeroom class will be made to stay after school with Joseph if he ignored my order and was deliberately late one more time. Well, I intend to keep my word. Every one of you will stay after school today. No exceptions. You can all thank Joseph for that! I'm sure you will."

He is back on death row! The action he feared most has become a hideous reality. In unison, Natalie and students of all three classes holler out, "It's not fair! We didn't do anything wrong! It's him, not us!" But Ms. Cunningham cuts them off. "I don't want to hear another word from any of you. You're all staying after school, and that's final!" The eyes of all his classmates are blazing back at Joseph, especially the toughest boys. "We'll get you," Frankie whispers loudly enough that the teacher must have heard his threat, but she ignores it. "Quiet! We will resume our lessons," she says. For the remainder of the morning, she did not call on Joseph even once, hardly looked his way.

At lunch, the teacher made sure that all the students had left her room and gone outside to the playground. Joseph takes his brown bag outside and eats his apple and banana around the corner of the building, out of sight. He'd seen his classmates gather together in a group on one side of the playground under the swings. An older boy, a lunchtime monitor from the higher grades seeks Joseph out. "Your classmates are planning to get you after school if that old Cunningham bitch makes everyone stay," he warns. "Watch out if you can. Go home a different route. Or call your father or mother to come and pick you up." Joseph thanks him for the warning. "What did you do to make that old Cunningham bitch hate you that much? It can't just be for being late to her class, can it?"

Joseph shakes his head as if he doesn't know the answer, but he thinks of Peter and the Hitler youth in Germany taunting and beating his friend after school. It isn't just lateness; something else is at work here. Given a reason, his classmates will surely pile on and attack him. In a strange way, Joseph feels extra punishment is due him. He notices that even his friend Dougie has turned away from him and joined the band of conspirators under the swings. Even in America, Joseph senses distrust if you are born of a different race or religion. No way he can easily fit in and be invisible like the others. Nor can his own parents, who seemed blind to it all. They were brought up in the Valley, a town ten miles away that is at least one-third Jewish and has the flavor of a European shtetl on summer nights, with friends and neighbors walking hand in hand down the middle of the street. His mother's family lives on a hill that the tough, uncouth kids call "Jew's hill," where his widowed Russian grandmother, Bubby Sarah, runs a boarding house and is president of the Cooperative. Most of his parents' friends from high school live there, and his father located his professional office in that shtetl-like town which is so close but seems to the boy to be in a far distant country. Yet they built their bungalow home on Grandfather's farm because it was economic to do so, and times were very bad. No one thought of the boy. They are in America, where everyone is supposed to meld together, or so they idealistically imagine. Schools are the same everywhere, a safe place where you go to learn, and no one is considered different or picked on or taunted unless he deserved to be. Besides, Joseph is never able to explain to them how different he feels or share the problems he gets into. Most of all, he is ashamed of himself for lacking the personality or character to overcome these differences. True, he doesn't wear a yarmulke or prayer beads or look that different. So he's come to feel it's his own fault—not for being born of a different religion, but for being unable to meld in. He has dark Mediterranean skin, but so do Italians and Catholics like Frankie. Yet there's no way he is able to fit in as easily as Dougie or almost any of the other Christian kids—no matter how stupid, mean, crazy, fat, or ugly they may be—even if he really loves baseball and is pretty good at it. So he's learned to keep to himself, and he tries to figure out a separate pathway of his own.

All afternoon, it is impossible for Joseph to concentrate on his workbook. His mind is churning so fast. Was last night's dream a forewarning that he'd be singled out and made a victim in school? Did his dream have hidden meaning beyond the threat of Bundsmen or Nazi armies invading and taking over their countryside? Maybe he was unconsciously aware of his teacher's Friday threat, and if so, why didn't he listen? Why didn't he wake up early and get to school on time? Was he, in some unconscious way, challenging her crazy threat to punish everyone? And why did Ms. Cunningham think to bring his classmates into it at all and incite them? It was her way of getting even with him for his disobedience, she said that. But what was it about him personally that offended her so much that she'd turn his lateness into something this awful? It seemed too personal, more than simply teaching him a lesson. "She's a frustrated old maid who's been ruler of her classroom forever," Mother explained after their school meeting. "She lives for her power in that classroom and she needs to have everything her way just like the nuns. She has tenure and doesn't have to worry about losing her job unless she or her sister actually poisons someone. I'd be proud to have an excellent reader like you if it was my class and have him help the others, not be antagonistic toward him." Mother thought his reading skill and lip-reading in class was the whole problem, but it was only a part. While insisting he play with blocks, draw and color in his workbooks, Ms. Cunningham was equally disturbed when he'd reached out and tried to teach first graders, like little Angelo, who had a real hard time reading and asked for his help. She'd strike out in anger whenever she caught him talking to Angelo. After that parent-teacher meeting, Joseph learned to clam up. His parents were likely to inflict a second whack or punish him in some way if he told them about having any more problems with his "difficult" teacher.

Meanwhile, Ms. Cunningham marked Joseph Satisfactory on his quarterly report card, except for behavior, punctuality, and attendance. She once claimed to mark all her students exactly the same, but big Natalie claimed that she got all Excellent and so did the cute little French girl.

Joseph recalled another time in the first grade when the teacher spoke with genuine passion about the struggle of English girls and boys forced to leave their homes and flee to the countryside for fear of German bombing raids, and tears started running down her face. She taught the class words to a popular English song from the Great War and had everyone sing along with loud rhythmic emotion. Then, out of the blue, Ms. Cunningham walked down the aisle and suddenly lunged out at Joseph, whacking him on the back of his head with her open palm, landing a stinging blow that really hurt him, and then she grabbed her own hand in pain. Joseph was stunned by the act; he had no idea why she struck him or what he'd done wrong. The teacher took a full moment to gather her emotions before shouting, "I don't want to see you bobbing your head like that in my classroom ever again! Back straight, chin up, and no more bobbing about like a tree full of chimpanzees in a zoo!"

The boy hadn't realized what he'd done wrong. Why was he bobbing? Only then did Joseph recall going to synagogue with his father and grandfather the week before on the High holy day of Yom Kippur where he had learned to sing out prayers alongside the grown-up men with shawls, beads, and yarmulkes on their heads, weaving back and forth into the night—all bobbing their heads and clapping their right hands to their breasts in unison, begging God to forgive all their peoples' sins before the book of life closed for the year. But why should his bobbing and weaving incite her? Joseph wondered. Was it the strangeness of his movements or is she what his Bubby calls, "an anti-Semite," who hates Jews and all their religious practices? The boy never dared tell his parents about the bobbing-and- weaving incident for fear of getting into deeper trouble by accusing her of this greater possible intolerance. But mostly because he is ashamed of himself, of his inability to please or even cope with this teacher at school. And it's so much more peaceful at home when he keeps these problems to himself.

While Joseph tried to be good and obey the teacher to avoid her disapproval, something always seems to come up that infuriates her, like his bobbing, asking too many questions, challenging an answer—or physical things, like not combing his hair, not properly cleaning his teeth or ears or just sitting down at his desk with mud on his pants from baseball slides in the playground. She was always finding things wrong with him and catching him by surprise. Clearly, the other kids got into trouble as well, but she seldom surprised them with that same level of unexpected anger and punishment. She was, of course, generally sweet to her personal favorites, big Natalie and the cute little French girl but even the loudest, dumbest kids, like Frankie and pinhead Conklin, suffered from her rage and ruler far fewer times than he did. Yet now, Ms. Cunningham is acting really out of line, taking her dislike of him a full step further. Joseph realizes she is doing something illegal, something that a good teacher would never do—setting all the students in her homeroom against one student. Against him!

The classroom clock clicks loudly as its hand jumps ahead to one minute before three o'clock. Joseph feels his throat seize up in panic. "Students waiting for the bell to end school is a good example of Einstein's relativity," his father once explained. "Waiting for that last minute of the school day may seem to take forever, but place your hand on the surface of a burning hot stove and you'll move it off in a flash closer to the speed of light." Today's last minute seems to take an eternity marked by absolute silence across the classroom.

"She won't do it. She can't. I'm sure she'll back down," Joseph whispers to himself louder than intended.

"She better not, or we'll cut your thumbs off!" Frankie warns, his garlic breath passing close behind Joseph's right ear.

Frankie has the dirtiest mouth in his class, but he can walk the talk, the older boys say. He's Sicilian, and from day one in first grade, he set out on his goal to get protection money—nickels, dimes, even pennies—from almost all the boys, and once or twice from a girl. Frankie's father, a day laborer, had hired out to help Joseph's grandfather redig their well a few years back. Though thin and wiry, Grandfather said he never met a man better at shoveling or swinging a pickax all day long without tiring. Frankie seems to resent Joseph all the more for his father's labor on the "Jew-farm" and corners him loudly so everyone can hear. "Why ain't you got no money? Steal it from your father's wallet. Everyone knows Jews got all the dough. Didn't Christ whip the ass of all the Jew moneylenders on the Temple steps and took all their filthy gold?" Moneylending was another reason to hate Jews, he guessed, although the biggest, most respected banks lend money, and Joseph never heard that the Pope said a nasty word against banks or bankers nor do priests turn bankers' money down at weekly collections. And what about Jews like Grandfather, land poor and without any money to lend, who is surviving the Depression by hard work—raising chicks in his incubator, selling eggs and chickens, milking his cow, and by farming and renting out his larger fields and sometimes hiring himself out for roofing or carpentry work. Joseph's father doesn't have much money either although he'd won scholarships and studied to become a physicist but the Great Depression began the year he graduated from Cornell, and who needs physicists in a depression? So he studied Law and Optometry to decide between the two and started his practice as an eye doctor in tough economic times when most people buy wire eyeglasses at the Woolworth five-and-ten-cent store. But Frankie once spotted Joseph's father going to work all dressed up in an unwrinkled suit and starched white shirt with a bow tie, and his gentlemanly appearance made Frankie desire to protect Joseph all the more. "Protect me from who?" Joseph asked him. Frankie said he told that to a Sicilian friend and his friend nearly split a gut laughing. There's an army of secret gangsters called the Black Hand over in Sicily and now in America that all the boys and girls are supposed to know about and be scared of. So most of them stay out of Frankie's way and claim to be penniless like every other good American Depression kid when he corners them in the coatroom and desires so badly to protect them.

The moment the bell rings to end the school day, the boys and girls in homeroom class jump up and start a mad rush toward the door. "Stop!" old Ms. Cunningham cries out in her nastiest snarl. "No one leaves until

I say you may leave. Let me remind all of you why you are to remain in your seats and be kept after school."

"Because stupid Joseph got to school late again," big Natalie cries out in disgust.

"No," the teacher said, "because some children, unlike most of you, have been brought up badly, ill trained, and refuse to listen to authority. We are all going to teach Joseph a lesson he'll never forget."

"But, Ms. Cunningham, my mom's waiting outside to take me to my piano lesson," big Natalie wails. Most kids chime in with excuses; everyone is remarkably busy with chores or has a doctor or dentist's appointment they must get to. While excusing no one at first, the kindly old teacher decides to let all her kindergarten kids go home since they are too young to teach Joseph a lesson, and besides, many have parents or neighbors waiting in cars outside. She then allows a few special first and second graders to leave, mostly girls, including her favorites, Natalie and the cute little French girl, because they practice too hard to be deprived of their weekly music lessons. "Attention! I want absolute silence," she shouts, smacking the well-made wooden ruler back and forth into the palm of her left hand. Joseph takes out a book and begins to read a story. "You! Put that book away," she yells. "You're the one being punished. Don't you get it? No books, no homework. Sit up straight. Shoulders back. I'll let you all know when Joseph's stay-after-school time is over!"

Joseph's classmates, most of them boys now, sit seething, while Ms. Cunningham ignores them and settles down comfortably at her desk to mark test papers. Just then, Mrs. Koch, the pretty third and fourth grade teacher comes to the door, but Ms. Cunningham waves her away. She nods sadly, as if aware of the unusual punishment situation at hand and knows not to interfere. Made to sit upright in the center of the front row, Joseph tries not to listen to whispered threats from Frankie and the angry boys behind him. The teacher must hear them too. She is not that deaf but she must have decided that letting them threaten him was part of his punishment. Joseph feels more and more like the powerless victim in his nightmare, unable to face up to or escape from the moment of impending crash by Nazi motorcyclists. But he's living in reality now, no way to wake up and make this nightmare end. The torture is Ms. Cunningham's doing, and it is so unfair, he's sure, like one of those immoral acts by Nazi SS that Peter never stops talking about when he comes to play. Joseph has always been troubled by one story in particular of the Nazis using immoral force against a whole village. He's not sure it's true because Peter can't recall the name of that little French village, which isn't like him.

The Nazis threatened to kill one man, woman, or child each day *in that small French coastal village until its townspeople turned over the resistance fighter who'd planted a bomb in their occupied town hall, which exploded and killed a Nazi soldier. The first and second day at noon, the Nazis shot two of the strongest men in town. On day three they executed the most vocal woman protestor, one of their wives. And on day four, the Nazis selected a five-year-old boy to be executed the following noon. But early that morning, two French villagers brought in the dead body of a man they said admitted to being the resister who planted the bomb. He was an old man, a blacksmith, who was said to be sick, suffering from throat cancer, and had less than six months to live. They'd killed him by mistake, the men said; they only meant to wound him when he mounted his horse and tried to escape. No one could be sure that the blacksmith was the true resistance fighter, but it hardly mattered. The Nazis made their point, which was to hold everyone in that village responsible and kill off the entire town if necessary for a resister's action against the Nazi occupation. Who cared if in the absence of a known resister, the French villagers took justice into their own hands and produced a dead body to satisfy their evil occupiers. Who could blame the two Frenchmen for killing this sick old man, if indeed, it was murder? They didn't create the rules. They simply played the game by the immoral Nazi rules and stopped the slaughter of their entire village. A scapegoat was needed, so they supplied one.*

Joseph's inescapable confrontation with his angry classmates is just minutes ahead, the moment his manipulative teacher decides to unlock the door and free her classes. Does she care what they'll do to him? Is it her cruel intention that they gang up and teach him a lesson about obeying her authority even if he winds up badly hurt? She probably enjoys the prospect of getting even with him, Joseph feels, although in her position, she can't be seen to enjoy it. Her face, as she sits there marking papers, reflects a determination to make them all suffer longer so they'll make Joseph suffer all the more. What did the gang of tougher boys plan at lunchtime when they met under the swings? Joseph can envision them pouncing on top of him but do they plan to hold him down while Frankie or someone tries to break his arm or leg or even pluck out an eyeball and blind him? Will they just use their fists, or will they go after him with clubs or with a baseball bat? Will Frankie pull out that Swiss army knife he once brought to school and try to cut his thumbs off? Isn't that what the Sicilian Black Hand does to their enemies? In a near panic, Joseph wonders whether he'll be strong enough to survive a gang beating even if they only use their hands or fists and boots to kick him. Was there anyone, any other teacher, who might try to stop them? No, the boy feels sure they won't attack him on school grounds. More likely, they'll grab him and drag him down by the railroad track siding or a clearing in the woods behind their winter ice pond. He'll be safe if he is able to stay close to the school, at least inside school grounds on the playground. Wendell, the janitor, will be at work a few hours more. But how long can he hope to hide out here before the boys come back to the school and get him?

Sensing their restless anger, Joseph sneaks a look behind him at their grotesque faces reflected in the high, double-glazed school windows; all eyes swing round to meet his gaze, except for Dougie, who looks away. There's not a friendly face left among them. Half an hour has passed, and still no sign that Miss Cunningham is about to let the class survivors go. The longer she keeps them imprisoned for Joseph's crime, the more their anger festers and their need for revenge will be greater. The boy feels like an animal caught in his teacher's trap with a pack of wolves gathering round gnashing their teeth. Panic rises from his belly into his throat; he swallows phlegm and tries to calm himself by imagining something worse.

What if he'd been the Nazi resister in that small French village who'd planted the bomb? Would he find the courage to turn himself in and stop the Nazi SS from murdering the kid and all the other townspeople, maybe his own parents or his new baby sister? Joseph tries to imagine he'd have that much courage, but he was pretty sure he wouldn't. Was it better to keep resisting or better to give himself up and be executed to stop the Nazi monsters' immoral killings of innocent fellow villagers? Thinking about this greater dilemma had a calming effect on Joseph. No telling what you'll do or how courageously you might act until you're truly faced with life or death. Anyone's a liar, he thinks, who tells you he's brave enough to face death. And if he were the resistance bomber, would the townspeople blame him and hate him for the horrible slaughter he is causing them? Would they curse him for not admitting his crime of resistance and giving himself up? Not likely that they'd honor his action or hate the Nazis any more for their unjust killings. No, more likely they'd blame him, beg him to stop resisting and turn himself in, like that crazed young Jewish boy who killed a German sub-ambassador in Paris and whose impulsive act led to Kristallnacht, the night of broken glass, with hundreds of Jews killed and arrested and all the Jewish temples in Berlin burned to the ground. While condemning the evil Nazis, some blamed the boy for his naive act of vengeance, which brought the Nazi horror down on all of them: "Why did he start up with them and give them an excuse to kill us?" Well, Joseph realizes that his classmates blame him completely; none blame old Ms. Cunningham for trying to teach him a lesson. He is squarely to blame; all he had to do was obey her order and get to school on time like everyone else. Unfair as her penalty is, they act as if the teacher had no alternative; they can't wait to gang up and take their frustrations out on him.

"Morality can turn all topsy-turvy," Peter once tried to explain to him. "Morality goes on a holiday when the powerful hold all the cards and change the rules. I swear, the Nazi devils turned a whole nation of mostly decent people against us! Can you understand that?" No, Joseph hadn't truly understood his friend's deeply felt views about Nazi immorality before, but he was beginning to understand now, trapped in his teacher's nasty punishment act and about to come face-to-face with the fury of his increasingly enraged classmates.

Fifty-five agonizing minutes have passed since the last bell; it's close to four o'clock when an expressionless Ms. Cunningham finally stands up to excuse what remains of her classes, announcing, "You may go now. I hope all of you have learned this lesson."

Joseph sits anxiously at his desk uncertain what to do next as he watches his freed classmates race into the hallway, hears them bolt out the front door and exchange loud shouts and curses as they enter the playground outside. The boy and teacher remain together in grim silence. Then a sharp sound as the classroom clock clicks off another long minute. Ms. Cunningham looks out in Joseph's direction, but the boy has made no sign of moving from his desk. Will she say anything at all, he wonders. He notices that the teacher does not confront him and ask, "Well, Joseph, have you learned your lesson?" Nor is she waiting for his contrite response, "Oh yes, I surely have, Ma'am." Instead, the teacher addresses the boy softly but with an underlying hostility. "You may not stay here in my classroom. I'm locking up right now." She knows her trap has been well-set, and his classmates are outside lingering around the schoolyard, waiting to confront Joseph. In her mind, it is all his fault. Hadn't she properly warned him? Who could possibly blame her for whatever might happen to the boy? Is she able to admit to herself that she doesn't really care? Not about that boy. He's too arrogant and undeserving, unlike the others who truly need her help. So plain old Ms. Cunningham stands at her door jiggling the keys from her pocketbook. Joseph finally shrugs his shoulders, rises to his feet, and stumbles out of her homeroom, barely noticing that she has stayed behind. The moment he exits the front door of the school, she will go to her car and drive home for a pleasant late-afternoon glass of wine or tea with her older sister. Perhaps she's thinking about the mashed potatoes and stew they eat five nights a week or of her favorite sponge cake, bread pudding, or custard dessert. Joseph knows there is no way on earth Ms. Cunningham is going to help him, nor is she in any way concerned about his physical well-being.

In the hallway, Joseph walks past the nurse's room, which has a telephone. The door is locked, but homeroom teachers are expected to open it if a student asks. Maybe he should call his father to come get him. But Father has office hours, and Monday afternoons may be a busy time.

His father would come get him if he lied and claimed to be sick, dizzy, or nearly passed out, thinking it might be appendicitis or something serious. But he'd be in for a beating if he lied to his father, and there was no way he'd admit the truth—that he was afraid to face his own classmates who are waiting outside to gang up and get their revenge. Anyway, he wasn't sure Ms. Cunningham would follow the rules and open the nurse's door to let him call his father. Well, he won't give her the satisfaction of turning him down. So the boy moves down the hall step-by-step to face up to his fate, afraid of the mob outside, but more afraid of how badly he might react in front of them.

The moment Joseph opens the schoolhouse door and walks down the steps, he is met by two older escorts from the seventh or eighth grades. "Come this way with us," they order, guiding Joseph by both his arms. "Your classmates are waiting. I think they want to walk you home." The boy sees he has no choice. They guide him out of the empty schoolyard to the top of the hill leading down to the railroad tracks. It all seems most frightening to Joseph and quite strange, more like a scene from a movie or part of a bizarre dream like his Nazi-blitzkrieg nightmare. Joseph feels extremely vulnerable. He's too young, not yet eight years old and a second grader; this kind of scary ambush should be happening to someone much older, at least a teenager. While the prospect of war has consumed him, he doesn't feel at all like a soldier now; he thinks of Peter and playing imaginative kid games as farmers or ranchers in his hilly backyard. Joseph feels his heart thumping fast and loudly; he's lucky that the bigger boys can't hear the sound of his heart, or they'd be mocking him for the cowardly sound of his heartbeat. He just prays to stay calm and not wet his pants or do something cowardly that will humiliate and haunt him for the rest of his life.

Held loosely by his arms, Joseph looks down from the crest of the hill to a sandpit fifty feet below along the railroad spur, where an anxious group of seven or eight boys and two or three girls are waiting. All so unreal! He feels like a prisoner in a movie he's seen, being marched down a hill to the guillotine in the French Revolution. No sense trying to pull away from the bigger boys, Joseph realizes; better to try to act calm, to make believe it's all happening to someone else. The mob of classmates and a few older boys are pacing about the sandpit below, waiting to attack. Joseph tries to slow the descent and study their faces one by one, but all the faces blur together into a fourteen-armed octopus, and the creature begins to yell out and curse him. "Here he comes, the yellow little asshole who made us all stay after school!" "Let's kill the sheeny kike!" yells his nemesis, Frankie. "Yeah, let's teach the fat little bastard a lesson he won't forget." "Hey, first, let's break the stinking Jew boy's arm!" Frankie hollers, making a loud snapping sound.

As Joseph approaches closer and closer, the group forms a half-circle around the sandpit, leaving an opening for their victim to enter. The two older escorts get directly behind Joseph and push him sharply forward into the center of the waiting creature. Joseph piles headlong into three or four boys, falling to his knees.

Instantly, he feels the enormous power of the mass as their force drives him headfirst into the sand. Fists begin punching at his head, and hard leather boots kick out at his ribs and groin under the pileup. Joseph hoped to meet his unfair destiny with at least some courage. Knowing he is about to get badly hurt or even crippled, he tries to imagine it being an impersonal pummeling, more like being smacked down in a football or rugby scrimmage. That's it, more like a rough game, except for the absence of an impartial referee ensuring the rules of the game. But all at once, fright takes over as Joseph's face is driven so deep into the sand by the weight of many bodies that for few seconds he's unable to catch his breath. He spits sand out from the corners of his mouth, works his jaw free, spits again, and manages to scream out, "Stop it! Stop it! I can't breathe!"

A moment later, he feels the great weight disappear as the two older boys pull Frankie, Kenny, and the others off his back. Joseph props himself up on one elbow, gasping for breath. Now he is frightened for his life as the four angriest classmates leap toward him, stomping about like giant hunting dogs, mouths foaming over to get at a fox, craving to dive back and resume pummeling and kicking him just as soon as the older boys step aside. Joseph's mind whirls frantically, seeking a safe space inside the eye of the hurricane. He fights off the temptation to let it all go and be transported back into the middle of his nightmare, paralyzed and helpless as the Nazi cyclists roar down the road about to drive their machines into him, ripping his body to shreds. Why not lie down and surrender? Give in to the anger and force of the mob? Yet instead of lying down and accepting their beatings, Joseph finds his voice, and he shouts out stammering, "Stop! Just stop it! I can't fight all of you at once! It's not fair!"

"Wait! What's not fair?" the taller escort asks, holding off the angry younger boys. "I'll fight them all," Joseph gasps out heroically, "but one at a time! It's not fair to have to fight everyone at once!"

"Who gives a shit about fair!" yells Frankie. "Just let me at the chicken shit little Jew bastard. I'll kill him!" "Yeah. Get out of our way!" Joseph then hears a girl whisper, "He's a Jew. Didn't you know that?" Afterward, Joseph will remember almost every curse word thrown at him, especially the Jew references, as if his angry classmates are trying to make him into less of a good old American country boy like them and turn him into an alien stranger who deserves punishment. But the taller escort is immovable, standing between Joseph and the mob.

"Just hold on! He says he'll fight all of you, but one at a time. I think that's fair. That makes sense to me."

Thank God, Joseph thinks, *maybe there are rules and a referee after all. Maybe I lucked into an older boy with a conscience.* He would always remember the taller escort's determined look and firm lantern jaw. Maybe one person can make a difference even when facing this mob of angry boys driven to enact the thrill of violent retaliation against a deserving classmate, an unwanted Jew boy at that.

"Okay, stand back. Let me at him first!" Frankie yells, tackling Joseph and driving him back down into the sand. Yet this time the other boys don't pile on; they hang back in a close-knit circle, urging Frankie to break a wrist, at least a finger, or push a thumb into his eyeball. One boy at a time, Joseph feels he has a chance of surviving. All piling on, they might badly hurt or even suffocated him by mistake, for he'd felt the superhuman force of four or five strong young bodies driving his head and nose deep into the sand. The panic that overwhelmed him has left; now he must find a way to protect himself and survive. So Joseph arches his body under Frankie, trying to find a position of strength. While his adversary is muscular and acts much tougher than the others, Joseph notices that he is actually the bigger one, with more weight. He begins to use his weight and manages to wrestle Frankie over on his side, turning his body little by little until Joseph is able to work his way on top of the tough Sicilian boy, pinning his shoulders.

"Hey! Come on, Frankie," Conklin yells. "You're letting the little Jew bastard beat you!"

In a strange way, their Jew cursing seems to give Joseph greater strength, as if the person they are cursing is not limited to him alone, with all his boyish fears and vulnerabilities, but to a stranger whose powers neither he nor they can be certain of. Meantime, Joseph manages to keep holding Frankie down in a position near a pin for so long that the crowd of avengers becomes restless; they move closer, circling round to whack Joseph on his shoulders and sting the back of his head with their fists. He catches sight of Dougie on the edge of the mob moving along with them, and he winces from the shame of his onetime friend's betrayal.

"Let them fight it out I told you!" the taller referee boy steps in and orders.

Tough as he is, like his macho hero Mussolini, Frankie can't wrestle Joseph's heavier body off him, and, frustrated, he screams out nonstop curse words aimed at inciting his gang. It works; the other boys become increasingly hostile, pushing past the would-be referee. "Damn it, Frankie needs a little help. Come on, let's all help Frankie!" Conklin hollers, and the boys shove Joseph off the top, reversing positions as Joseph's hopes for a fair fight with a referee evaporate. *No, they can't let it be fair. They're out for my blood.* Once again, Joseph uses all his strength and superior weight to turn the tough, snarling boy over on his back and slowly works his way atop his writhing enemy and into pin position. But the mob won't let him stay there. The boys come to Frankie's rescue again, forcing Joseph off the top; this time, someone wrenches his left arm behind his back, bending it until he feels it might actually break. *It's all hopeless,* Joseph sees. *No way they are going to let me win.*

A survival strategy takes shape in Joseph's young mind. He arches his back like a turtle and lets Frankie slide on top and try to turn him over. The turtle position takes less than Joseph's full strength to keep the tougher boy from turning him and doing real harm. Frankie is cursing again; he starts to whack Joseph on the back of his head, but the boy senses his strategy might be working. In an eerie way, Joseph feels almost safe from the angry mob while in turtle position in the sandpit with Frankie on top unable to turn him. All the while, Frankie is cursing him with every anti-Jew epithet his gutter mind can muster. The boys have been wrestling back and forth in that stalemate position for five or ten minutes. Joseph prays that his classmates will get tired or bored with the fight, seeing that the small, tough Italian Black Hand can't hurt him badly when the fight is a more even one-on-one. Yet Joseph fears Frankie may be more of a marathon runner than a sprinter. Like his laborer father, he may be able to wrestle all afternoon, never tiring, and wear Joseph out by nightfall. And even if Joseph survives Frankie, there are still three other angry classmates hanging over him, waiting for their chance at revenge, including Kenny, the strongest boy in their class. Joseph finds it's safest to hang on to Frankie and act like he's straining to work his way out from under, but he is actually conserving his strength for there is no telling how long their wrestling match might last or what surprise the avengers would hit him with next. So far, they haven't used a baseball bat, a rock, or Frankie's much-feared Swiss army knife.

"Mr. Matthews is coming!" an older boy screams out. Mr. Matthews is a young substitute teacher for the higher grades who is also doubles by teaching physical education. Joseph doesn't really know the man or know what to expect, but he remembers Matthew's face as constantly frozen in an amused half-grin. "Okay, m'boys, what do we have going on here?"

"Nothing much," the taller referee boy says. "The little kids are having a wrestling match, that's all."

Mr. Matthews looks at the group of ten or so and shakes his head in disbelief. "I could hear you from my room, cursing and shouting for the last twenty minutes," he says. "That's long enough for any wrestling match, I think. Okay, let's break it up, boys."

Frankie acts like he didn't hear the teacher, so Mr. Matthews has to reach down and pull him off by his hair, and Frankie begins to curse him too. Joseph's eyes meet the teacher's, and he thinks he sees a flash of sympathy. Or is it pity for his shame? *Whatever, maybe there is a God in Heaven watching over us after all,* Joseph thinks, trying to brush away all the sand that has gotten under his jacket and shirt, into his underpants and down into his socks and shoes.

"Hey! You're the winner, Frankie boy," gangling Conklin shouts. "You pinned him twice." "Bullshit! I'm not done with that yellow little Jew bastard yet! All he does is hang on to me like a girl, so I can't really hurt him."

Acting like a good shepherd or herd dog, Mr. Matthews, the always grinning phys ed teacher, leads a whittled down herd of six boys plus Joseph, guiding them across the tracks and down the sloping road past their winter skating pond and then up the hill into the small village center. The teacher stops on the sidewalk corner of Main Street across from the country store and orders the herd of frustrated boys to disperse. Slowly, one or two at a time, the boys move off in seemingly different directions. Joseph stands there uncertain, telling himself to remain calm, wondering if he should make a run for it across the street toward his home, a mile or so up the hilly country road. He hesitates a moment more, thinking about following Mr. Matthews into the safety of the grocery store.

Too late! The second Mr. Matthews turns his back and enters the community market, the four toughest classmates regroup and surround Joseph. With Mr. Matthews and the tall referee boy out of the picture,

Frankie and the three other boys are not about to give up their chance to avenge themselves on the pariah who caused their teacher to punish them. They corner Joseph on Main Street and jostle him into an open lot and onto a grassy patch behind a row of bushes in the rear of the insurance office owned by Dougie's father. Frankie is aching to continue the fight where he left off, but Kenny insists it's his turn. Kenny, a usually likable Polish boy, has wavy blond hair and is lean, big for his age, and has a hawklike grace, the best athlete in their class. Earlier this year, his first at school, Kenny was taunted by Frankie since the German forces—with "secret help" from their Italian allies, he claimed—had humiliated the weak Polish army by beating them so quickly and decisively with their Nazi blitzkrieg of Stuka planes, panzer tanks and artillery that it was embarrassing. While Poland, the country, hadn't fared well in its war with the Germans, Kenny wasn't the least embarrassed. In fact, he rose to the challenge and gave tough little Frankie a boxing lesson and a badly swollen right eye. "Stop looking at me! My eye ain't hurtin' that bad!" Frankie stomped about, raving mad. Kenny's two older brothers, it seems, taught him how to defend himself, so the schoolyard battle between Italy and Poland went clearly to the Polish side, although Frankie never actually gave up. He just stopped—'cause he couldn't see too clearly where he left his bag an' stuff. So when Kenny says it's his turn to fight Joseph, Frankie is more than willing to step aside and enjoy watching his hawklike young Polack friend bash the grubby little Jew's head in.

Kenny begins to circle Joseph with his arms extended, showing off his ring style, about to give the gang another lesson in the gentlemanly art of pugilism. Kenny is up on his toes, dancing, pummeling the boy with jabs that sting when they land on his mouth or ears or on the side of his head. Joseph tries to think of a strategy to cope with this greater force. He goes into a bearlike crouch, remembering reading about a chunky little foreign boxer who'd almost gone the distance with Joe Louis, "the Brown Bomber." Joseph tries to block Kenny's jabs, taking punches on his arms, elbows, or shoulders and ducking his head. He tries to flail back, though awkwardly, whenever he is stung. Their one-sided stylish dance ends suddenly when Kenny leaps forward and smashes the boy directly on the bridge of his nose, and blood spurts out and runs down Joseph's good shirt and onto his jacket sleeves when he brushes them across his face. The small group of avengers find true rhythm now, beginning to clap and cheer in sync, having a real good time revenging themselves at Joseph's expense. While Kenny keeps his fast boxing tempo up in rhythm with the cheering crowd, he seems a bit reluctant to step in forcibly again and try for a knockout. Meantime, Joseph is having a difficult time catching his breath with blood running into his mouth. He feels shame as tears run down both his cheeks; he desperately wants to stop, to give up, but he cannot give in to them. He knows they won't let him off that easily. Two others, Charley and the gangling Conklin kid, are still waiting for their turn, and Frankie can't wait for a second chance. So bloody-nosed and breathing badly through his mouth, Joseph doesn't quit as an agile, ever-intense Kenny keeps circling, jabbing at the boy's swelling nose and battered face. *Why won't they stop and leave me alone? Haven't I been hurt enough to learn whatever lesson these beatings are supposed to be all about?* His classmates' need to inflict greater punishment seems to Joseph to have crossed a line and become sinful in its own right; their revenge has gone well beyond the old maid teacher's spiteful lesson and into something much more personal—an act of vengeance that has touched an atavistic streak in these schoolboys, who are clapping and howling like hunting dogs for more and more of his blood. How much will be enough? Joseph gasps, as he swallows another glob of blood from his damaged nose.

"Whoa, boys! Hold fast there!" A thin, white-haired old gentleman in a worn brown suit and tie steps out of the back door of the insurance office for a smoke, and seeing the boys fighting, he steps onto the grassy patch right between them. One of Kenny's sharp jabs hits the older man on his extended arm and shoulder, and the young boxer steps back apologetically. "Sorry." The old man rubs his arm. "Not bad." He grimaces then smiles warmly at blond, hawklike Kenny. "You sure look like the winner to me." He turns to Joseph, thinking the battle is voluntary, and laughs. "Hey, little guy, you've donated enough blood? Save some for your country, m'boy."

Frankie steps up, desperate to keep the battle going. "Hey, Mister! Our teacher made us all stay after school because of him being late. She told us to teach him a lesson."

"Which teacher was that?" the older man asks quizzically. None of them answers. Joseph feels shame as his classmates try to explain to the insurance man that they are only doing their school's duty by teaching "the fat kid" a needed lesson about obedience and punctuality. But when they are done explaining, the older man nods and turns to Joseph, "Where do you live, son? Which way is home?"

The boy points westward, across the street beyond the majestic county courthouse. "Up Hempstead a mile or so."

"All right. You can go home now," the thin old gentleman orders in a surprisingly deep, commanding voice. "Fight's over, boys. We're all gonna let this young fellow go home now and get himself cleaned up and tended to." He nods at Joseph, lighting up another Camel cigarette. "Go on home, boy. It's safe. I'll be watching from the back porch here."

Joseph wants to thank the insurance man, but his nose is bleeding so profusely that he finds it hard to talk. To stop the blood, he tears off an edge of a school test paper that was in his jacket pocket and stuffs it awkwardly into his nose. The insurance man motions him to get on with it and leave. Joseph feels a sense of lightness, the weight of his punishment lifted. Unlike the hopelessly brutal Nazi Germany that his friend Peter can't stop talking about, America seems full of good, fair-minded people out to help one another. First, the tall boy referee, then the ever-grinning physical education teacher, Mr. Matthews, and now this wily old insurance agent puffing away at his smoke. People like his old maid schoolteacher, Ms. Cunningham, are the exception not the rule, manipulating his classmates and turning them against him out of pure spite. Yes, someone should report her. She should be disciplined, the boy thinks, maybe put on probation or even fired for setting them on him. She's like that police dog owner who ordered his guard dogs to attack a neighbor's kid on Halloween Hell Night. Didn't they fine him and send him to jail?

Crossing the green courthouse lawn, Joseph runs past its heroic bronze statue with scales proclaiming equal justice for all. He looks back across the street before ducking through the entry hedges into Dutch gardens. The white-haired old gentleman has placed his arm across Kenny's shoulder, and they are laughing together like good old buddies, neither looking in his direction. Joseph wonders what happened to the others—Frankie, Charley, and the gangly Conklin kid. He decides he'd better move quickly in a circuitous route through the well-planned garden pathways, and he comes out of the maze near the main service entrance to the county jailhouse. A heavyset black man in uniform is loading laundry bags into the back of an official-looking white Chevy truck. Joseph shifts his head sideways as he passes so the prison guard won't see his bloodied nose and shirt, but the guard hardly notices him. He slides down a neatly cut grass bank to the edge of a gentle hillside stream, whose water is so clear that you can see the shape and colors of its smooth stones on the bottom. He pauses a moment to wash blood off his face with the fine, cool, nearly drinkable water. Most of the bleeding has stopped now, but he feels intense pain and swelling on the bridge of his nose and wonders if it might be broken. The boy leaves the stream and begins to jog, circling through the woods around what was once a choppy baseball diamond until he approaches a densely bushed incline rising to a cliff, which is a shortcut leading to his county road. Making his way up to the cliff is a slow process due to its steepness and rows of thick, prickly bushes.

Halfway up the incline, Joseph is startled to hear echoes of human voices. He stops to listen, holds his breath, hoping the voices are coming from the distant, barred jailhouse windows. No, they sound more like boys' voices, but looking back all seems calm and serene. Then Joseph sees three shadowy figures moving toward him from the far side of the county jail. *No! They can't still be coming after me, can they?* He wants to move more quickly, but the going is rough as he edges his way through the thick, coarse bushes toward the cliff. Joseph now hears the breathless yelling of boys echoing from the cluster of trees below. He dares not stop to look but keeps trudging toward the crest, his body bent low and shifting right and left. Suddenly, he is startled to hear a stone hit the bushes near him across from his left shoulder. A second stone hits a few yards below his feet. Joseph moves more quickly, darting from side to side to make himself a harder target for his enemies. A sense of panic comes over him. No, this can't be happening. It seems unreal that Frankie and the other two boys are still chasing after him like bloodhounds and won't stop until they catch him. Will they follow him all the way home to his front door? What can be driving them so hard? Is it Sicilian Black Hand code to never stop pursuing a victim until you've gotten a full measure of revenge? Having climbed within a few feet of the crest, Joseph stops and stares down at his three attackers, trying to read their faces to determine how far they might go to hunt him down and really try to hurt him.

Frankie, along with Charley and crane-like Conklin, are encamped alongside a rock pile at the base of the hill about thirty yards below; one after another, the avengers scream out curses as they hurl angular stones, most golf ball size or larger, at his ascending form. This sudden hail of stones from the gang of young hunters seems like another weird fantasy to Joseph—a throwback to an ancient world of demons, witches, Satan and fears of afterlife in Hell. Where did these schoolboys get the crazy idea to start throwing stones? He tries to gauge the level of anger in their crazed heads. If he were down there alongside them next to the rock pile, would they really try to stone him to death? He feels their tempo increasing in its bitterness and need to inflict more harm. Can they hate him that much? Or is a deeper force driving them, an evil blood sport transported across time from primitive man's hunting or warrior nature? Is their hatred driven further by the recent outbreak of anti-Semitism toward Jews, from the ancient pyres of the Spanish Inquisition to today's burning crosses of Bundsmen or Nazi youth hunting down and attacking young Jews like Peter across Europe? Joseph senses evil forces at work here far deeper than he can imagine as his avengers hurl stone after stone, screaming out wildly with each throw. He stands on the cliff bewildered by his schoolmates' depth of hatred and passion; his anxiety deepens as their stones fall closer, like meteors across ancient hostile skies.

The boy's mind flashes back to an ancient desert image. Was it from a dream or a movie he'd seen? He is part of a mob in robes, stoning a teenage girl who has broken one of God's sacred commandments, carried away in lust by her married cousin. The girl's screams echo across the night sky; he sees sudden spots of blood on her long brown hair and smells the odor of the mob's sweaty bodies. Stone in hand, he follows along as the screaming girl falls to the ground, her forehead bashed open by the thud of a sharp stone. Whose stone was it? He is drawn along with the robed mob as it moves by the girl, hurling their stones long after the ghost has departed, leaving her contorted body in a nearby pit. Two old women remain to drag her lifeless flesh out of the pit. Feeling neither sadness nor remorse, the boy grips the sharp stone in his calloused young hand and hurls it with all his force at the three figures rising from the pit. But his stone seems to pass through them as if in a different dimension of time. Nor do the women seem to notice him as they drag their tiny young girl away from her place of earthly judgment—off to face the Devil and the fires of Hell?

Joseph feels a shudder of dark wings as images of this brutal ancient stoning travel across time and draw him into its horror. He feels guilt and personal shame for his own presence at the young girl's stoning. For one eerie moment, he imagines himself linked to this girl, a victim of injustice committed in an ancient lifetime. As if the scales of eye-for-an-eye justice have come round in time and are made whole again by his classmates' revengeful stoning in this, a future generation. How crazy a thought!

Joseph stands motionless on the crest of the hill, staring down at his classmates turned enemies, and a stubborn anger rises within him. He will not run any farther. So far, none of their stones has hit him or come close, and their vengeful energy begins to fade as their missiles fall harmlessly short of the target. With a frantic throw, Frankie's last stone sails higher, straight toward Joseph's head. The boy reaches out to catch it and the stone hits the center of his left palm, stinging him, then falls at his feet. Joseph picks up the stone. For all its evil intent, it is a smooth white stone half the size of a baseball, and a tactile pleasure runs through the boy's hands and shoulders as he rubs it between his palms and feels the warmth of the stone. Instinctively, he is about to hurl the missile back at them with all his force, but the image of that ancient stoning flashes before him. He stops. A slight smile crosses Joseph's face as he watches his tormentors back away then scurry off toward the far side of the county jail and the village beyond, and the sound of their cursing fades in the wind. Well, he stood his ground and their attacks have ended. He survived and should feel relieved; instead, he feels sunken, hollow inside.

A still moment in time. Soon it will be nightfall. Joseph feels the dark wings shudder once more as a large shadow falls across the cliff's crest. Feelings of anguish he's never felt before rise from the pit of his stomach and tear at his chest. Joseph has never felt more abandoned, more alone and rejected than at this moment in time. He stares at the smooth white stone thrown at him in bitterness and anger with the hope of cracking open his skull. How unreal! How truly alienated he must be for these schoolboys to come so far to hunt him down, stone, and curse him. And why does the stoning affect him so profoundly, he wonders, more than the fights and beatings? No, it wasn't the hail of stones themselves, which were mostly ineffectual. Something else: the feeling that he'd had a brief peak under the flap of an ancient carnival tent that contained a world of dark emotions far greater than he ever imagined, all part of a tidal wave of senseless evil screeching out across the centuries to wound and destroy millions of helpless little people of his race and other races. He sees himself as one more in a long chain of victims, an outcast, abandoned by his classmates, chased off into the wilderness like the holy day scapegoat to die its lonely death. Joseph feels alone and off-balance, as if planet Earth had ever so slightly changed its orbit and would never quite rotate the same way again. He fights these shadowland feelings, trying to stay upbeat and positive like Grandfather. Sure, hadn't he managed to stand up to his classmates' angry attacks and endure? Yet it was a hard lesson to learn that not a single boy or girl in his entire class took his side; he has no true friends there anymore; not one he can trust.

The boy shudders when he thinks about tomorrow. It will be hell on earth to return to school tomorrow and be forced to sit in class next to his tormentors, having felt their evil joy in punishing him. How can he face them and act as if nothing happened? Can he ever go over to Dougie's house anymore and ask him to play? Joseph feels what his friend Peter must have felt, with his bags packed, ready to embark on the merchant ship that will carry them across the turbulent Atlantic Ocean, driven from the land of his birth by countrymen turned strangers who had turned violently against him and his family of kind, generous, peace-loving doctors. No wonder Peter is so quiet and withdrawn, as if afraid to assert himself in America and simply *exist* like anyone else. Instead, he acts as if he is partly invisible, ashamed to cast his own shadow. Old gaptooth Thomas will later preach to him, "Just another lesson in how insignificant we really are and how little we can expect from all but a handful of good men and women. Remember," he says, "even our Lord Jesus was crucified on earth for our sins." A sad lesson that now haunts Joseph profoundly.

The worst is over; the best is yet to come. As Joseph begins a long slow walk up the hilly road toward home, his mind's eye continues to play tricks on him. Nightmare images of war and destruction gather in a cloud and proceed down the road toward him. In these twilight hours, they are unreal, ghostly reflections, an army of shadowy gray phantoms that pass him by without acknowledging his presence as their endless columns march down the road in the opposite direction and in another dimension of time. All the way home to the property line of Grandfather's farm, the boy walks past this phantom army of gray Nazi storm troopers, motorcyclists, trucks, artillery and panzer tanks. Relegated to this spectral dimension, they hold no terror for the boy as they float silently past him toward the county courthouse and village center. They are, perhaps, prescient beings, shadow creatures from a future time who one day may invade their village and destroy nearly everyone and everything in their wake, including an empty two-story wooden schoolhouse and a nearby rose cottage, where two old maids are taking after-dinner tea. Whatever will happen or when, this phantom army has its own agenda, not his; they have a world to conquer before they too will be met by a greater force and crushed.

Joseph's anxiety is about tomorrow, no longer about war or a Nazi invasion. Tomorrow is Tuesday. He must find the courage to get to school and confront them all tomorrow morning. Except he won't be late tomorrow. He's learned that lesson. Yes, old Ms. Cunningham is the winner as she knew she'd be. Joseph will get to school on time tomorrow morning despite a badly swollen nose and bruises on his face, and some of his avengers will laugh and mock him. Dougie will turn away, ashamed; his silence meant consent. Ms. Cunningham may try to ignore him too; maybe she won't be able to meet his eyes and acknowledge her role, knowing the beatings were all her doing through the actions of her loyal student attack dogs. Or maybe she'll simply smile to herself, content to feel her secret powers to inflict pain on those who don't obey her. "Whatever, I must learn to be patient," Joseph tells himself. "In less than a year, I'll be out of her clutches forever." He is determined to make it through the school year one step at a time, as gaptooth Thomas preaches. Things won't be the same for him at school without a friend he can trust, but brighter days lie ahead, he truly believes, if only he can make it past these frustrating early schoolboy years into adulthood. Grown-ups seem so much more reasonable and decent, and they abide by the law. Grown-ups don't go around beating each other up, at least not unless their nations declare war. Joseph begins to worry whether he'll ever find a girl who'll be true to him and won't betray him, or if he'll ever find friends and coworkers he can really trust. He wants to believe that when he grows up, decency will rule, and total strangers will try to be nice, generous, and easy to deal with. There will be much less violence in the air unless the Nazis and Fascist Bundsmen win the war and all hell breaks loose for Jews and everyone else in the civilized world.

By the time Joseph approaches his grandfather's farm, the Nazi phantom army has disappeared; he didn't notice exactly when. The boy stops and waits patiently across the street, allowing a large empty coal truck to roar down the steep road recklessly at a very high speed. As it passes, he sees the driver's wild, unshaven young face leering out at him. Once the runaway coal truck rattles out of sight, the macadam road is clear of all danger, safe up and down as far as the boy can see.

Joseph enters his bungalow home quietly, slipping past the baby's room and into the bathroom unseen. Locking the door, he tries as best he can to wash his bruised face and clean his bloody shirt. Joseph knows he cannot tell his parents what has happened. "All his fault," they will say. "He could have avoided it." Well, why didn't he? Was there some kind of demon inside him intent on challenging that old maid schoolteacher's authority? Like when you know you're about to do something bad, but you go right ahead and do it. Shouldn't he have remembered to wake up early and be at school on time since she'd been furious and announced her warning the prior Friday? He knows his parents will turn it all upside down and end up blaming him if he tells them and become very angry, as if they are responsible for his bad behavior. The teacher is always right, they say, even this Nun-trained teacher of "character." And they are probably right, he admits to himself; there was a part of him that refused to give in to her. Until, like a ringmaster's wild pony, she broke him.

The second his parents see Joseph's badly swollen nose and bruised face and see that he's been in a fight, they get upset. His mother yells out hysterically when she sees the wet shirt on the bathroom sink, says he's ruined one of the best shirts she ever bought him. Father acts furious too. He pulls off his belt to strap Joseph for fighting but stops after three or four sharp leather whippings. The boy acts surprisingly calm, doesn't protest or cry out, but takes the licking. He's right not to tell them about being late or Ms. Cunningham's Nazi-like punishment scheme that created a mob of vengeful classmates who gathered at the sandpile to ambush him with hatred, curses, and a physical beating beyond anything his parents in their adult innocence might imagine. They think Joseph simply disobeyed them and got into a fight with another boy. Both boys are usually at fault. Father, the pacifist, preaches to him that he doesn't have to fight anyone; it's best to turn your other cheek and walk away—the same lesson that gaptooth Thomas says his savior Jesus preaches. "You can't fight the world. Stupid to try." It strikes Joseph as odd his father citing Jesus. Did he sense the fight had something to do with his son's Jewishness? No, they don't think that way. Living in communities of fellow Jews all their lives, they don't have a clue what it's like to be the only Hebrew kid in school. All their friends are in that shtetl-like town miles away where both had gone to high school and where Father has his practice. And they're not children but grown-ups, which makes everything easier and provides a far different perspective for their innocence. There's no way he can talk to them about such things. This is America, they'd say. Grandfather purchased the farm and they built their bungalow home here. The nearest they'd come to his experience was the day the Fascist Bundsmen marched by threateningly, and they'd gone off with the baby to Bubby Sarah's house, leaving Joseph with Grandfather to face them. But it isn't his parents' fault if his schoolmates turned on him; he's the guilty one, a boy foolish enough to dare challenge his vicious teacher.

Right after Father's lesson, they send him to bed without dinner as punishment, which is fine with Joseph for he feels more physically tired and beaten than he's ever felt before. In the next room, the baby has fits of crying throughout the night from her hospital infection. But there are no Nazi nightmares, nor does he fall into a deep-Indian sleep. In fact, Joseph barely sleeps at all. His mind keeps racing off from its starting line faster than the speed of sound, he feels, recreating the ambush at the sandpit and his fistfight on the grassy patch, but mostly, the three boys chasing him up the hill with their hail of stones and outpouring of hatred. It is this image of punishment by stoning from ancient times that keeps rattling through his young mind, disturbing him, the sense of being driven like that scapegoat into the wilderness to die. Joseph is still wide awake when the roosters cackle at dawn. Only then does the boy fall into a sudden deep sleep, holding the smooth stone half the size of a baseball in his right hand tight against his chest and shoulder. But the following morning, he wakes up in plenty of time for school, and Father drives him. Joseph steps out into the school playground, determined to keep to himself and take it one step at a time. All that school year, he keeps the smooth stone at home on the side table near his bed. He will often roll it back and forth across his palms to feel its warmth when loneliness or scapegoat memories, new or old, return to haunt him.

The black-ink Nazi arrows in the newspaper halt at land's end to Grandfather's delight, reluctant to blitzkrieg across the English Channel and invade Great Britain. The old man is upbeat. Unlike the others, he laughs out loud at Joseph when he sees the boy's battered face and calls him our Shayner Yid, which is an old immigrant joke identifying a poor horror of a man named Penka by everything physically wrong with him as, "You know him, a beautiful Jew!" And, for the first time that week, Joseph can't help but break out laughing too.

Grandfather never asks him what happened. Grandfather has seen a lot of real tragedy. His own father was mugged and killed in the streets of New York when he was young; even worse, perhaps, his beloved teenage daughter fell victim to the influenza epidemic of 1918 and all they could do was sit at her bedside to comfort her and watch her die. So the old man can laugh at Joseph's Shayner Yid nose and face and put it all into perspective. We must move on from our setbacks. "Think of the Jewish boys your age in my homeland, Poland," he says unexpectedly. "Think of all the Fascist brutality they must be facing now every day of their lives." Which was pretty much the same idea as gaptooth Thomas's lesson about the man who complained about the pain in his foot until he met a man with one leg. Or Father's relativity.

Joseph survives the school year, despite old Ms. Cunningham's eagerness to punish him, by staying home sick whenever he deep-Indian sleeps too late. He pretends to be ill, learns to mask his healthiness by throwing up with a finger down his throat or manipulating the thermometer's temperature by use of a radiator or boiling hot water. But he tries to read a good book and look up words in the dictionary on those days he is absent. Over the school year, Joseph learns to live with his classmates' taunting and has few fights, mostly Frankie inflicted, but never again against all his classmates at the sandpile level of hatred and violence. That next fall, Joseph graduates to the pretty third and fourth grade teacher, Mrs. Koch's homeroom, safely out of old maid Cunningham's embittered grasp. She passes him in the hallway without a glance, as if he no longer exists, which is good!

All prewar hostilities are eclipsed that following December day when President Roosevelt declares war on Japan after its surprising attack on Pearl Harbor, then on Germany and Italy. Mrs. Koch's whole class seems to turn a page, looking outward beyond their schoolhouse walls as the entire nation pulls together. We are all Allies now in our fight for survival against the powerful Axis forces. He will witness no more threatening German-Bundsmen neofascist marches, and very few hungry, unemployed men walk the roads at dawn or raid their chicken coops. Even most anti-Semitism seems to have backed off and burrowed underground for the duration, except for Frankie, of course, who can't stop calling Joseph names. But the other kids hiss at him, and Kenny makes him flinch by labeling him "a Dago suck-up to his crazy fuckface uncle Adolph."

Tragic worldwide events take the place of personal animosities. The little French girl's uncle and his family disappear from a town along the Belgium border. Mrs. Koch and the third and fourth grade children get together to try to comfort her when she returns to school. The boys' curse words now focus on the "Nazis, Dagos, and sneaky Japs" as dangerous subhuman races as they once cursed Kikes and Niggers. Macho boys pray that war be long lasting, bragging that they can't wait until they're seventeen or eighteen, and able to join the US Army or Marines, be issued automatic weapons and grenades to blow the Nazi and Jap bastards to Hell. Joseph joins in their desire to kill Nazis and Japs rather than be killed. Yet he can't help but remember when those same subhuman curses were aimed at him, when their vision of him was clouded in prejudice—a dark-skinned alien boy with a yarmulke, beads, and strange religious practices whose ancestors crucified God's only son. While accepted as one of them now, he cannot share their subhuman imagery. How easily they might turn again at war's end when America is victorious, and the worst of them return to arrogant, time-tested prejudices and their ancient, predictable scapegoats once more.

When war begins, Joseph's aunt, a nurse, and her husband-to-be doctor volunteer and go off to war, his aunt to North Africa to help nurse the first group of American Army forces who are suffering fierce casualties in their early battles. Friend Peter keeps up with reports from the old country, tells the boy of reported gatherings and transports east by railroad of Jews from Germany and Austria. Their contacts in Europe warn of thousands sent off to concentration camps and of murderous firing squads in which hundreds of Jewish men, women, and even children are assassinated—made to undress then shot in the head from behind and buried in huge shoveled pits in hidden forests—a scale that was difficult for Grandfather to believe, even of the brutal Nazis. Joseph and his classmates work together on common war causes. They collect tin cans, scrap metal, and aluminum foil. They help in war-bond drives, join the Cub Scouts and learn to march, and play war games in forest thickets with BB guns instead of playing baseball on neatly cut diamonds or emerald green grass lawns. Joseph helps his grandfather as air-raid warden, running up and down the country road to nearby farm neighbors to check that everyone's window shades are black and no light peeks through during air-raid drills. He memorizes the distant silhouettes of US and enemy fighter bombers as he once memorized planets, stars, and constellations in the heavens with their wondrous Greek mythological names and imagery. "Every generation in the twentieth century has had its World war, for the peacemakers have been weak, powerless, and always fail us," Grandfather reads from one of his antiwar pamphlets. "So we are left to fight our generation's war or try to survive as civilians, although the stakes grow higher as technology's inhuman, long-range killing power takes great strides forward."

Joseph steels himself for the moment when he and his classmates are destined to match their courage and willpower against fierce Nazi youth trained from their swastika cribs for war. He envisions a scene when, as eighteen-year-old US Army privates, they will face a dozen real Nazi motorcyclists and armored troops on an Alpine mountain road, and their platoon must destroy them from ambush to survive. Old gaptooth Thomas's prophetic warning rings through his head. "To know the future, consult your fears!" It was a time to grow up quickly and prepare for the worst war imaginable. War is called Hell, but some of his macho classmates see it as their generation's great test, a chance to be heroic and save the lives of good army buddies or sexy teenage girls with ripped dresses or even risk death to rescue scared little kids whose parents got slaughtered. All of which Peter calls stupid and naive, reminding him of Hitler youth's warlike aspirations that lead his entire generation down a garden path to brutal, uncivilized killing and destruction. Joseph disagrees but says nothing. Killing can't be wrong if you're the one attacked and you are forced to defend yourself rather than surrender or be killed, as his grandfather was prepared to do had Bundsmen trespassed into their farmhouse. Well, in Peter's Germany, maybe they had no choice but to give in because nearly everyone had become Nazis or Nazi sympathizers. But that will never happen here in America. Joseph gazes at his shirtless image in the mirror and flexes the trace muscles that are beginning to develop on his arms and shoulders. He refuses to accept the anxiety-wracked face of a helpless young Jewish boy. No! He wills himself to no longer be powerless; he must grow up and prepare for the worst in a world gone mad with Nazi youth trained to be killer attack dogs. Joseph watches the glass darken as the afternoon sun moves slowly across the western sky, and his mirror image takes on a strangely mature, callous look, devoid of all expression, which he regards as a good start.

———

Time Chords

Memory is captured, contained in time chords, some of which soar and inspire our spirit, while others may dwarf us and claw at our beings for a lifetime. Living each moment with our memory music, both harmonious and discordant, we listen as our time chords play out their tunes—a soundtrack accompanying our most profound thoughts and raw emotions as long as we are alive with breath and powerless to escape their tenacious grip on our souls.

Joseph keeps the smooth rock from his childhood stoning, often calling upon its ancient powers and surprising warmth to help assuage the wounds of his most painful, anguished, loneliest moments. As a man, he travels across the globe consumed by the pressures of a rigorous life of challenging work and complex passions, and he turns less to the warmth of the stone until one day he notices it has vanished. Gone, along with a scatter of angular stones gathered one rainy afternoon at Stonehenge and a chip, hardly more than a pebble, taken from a crevice in the Western Wall in Jerusalem, site of the second Temple, intending to place it one day on his grandfather's graveside monument.

Over the years, Joseph stops to watch the boy standing on a crest, looking down at the hate-filled faces of his classmates as their shower of rocks fall short, all but the last stone, and the echo of their Christ-killer taunts are swallowed by the roar of cosmic winds. For the thousandth time perhaps, Joseph watches the boy pick up the smooth stone and rub it between his palms, creating a warm, calming friction. The boy marches through a phantom army that surges past in a fifth dimension as he makes his way up the country road toward Grandfather's farm and the bungalow his elders built that his family called home for twelve of his early years. Today, the wooden buildings remain, antique fortresses with leaky roofs and faulty plumbing surrounded by hundreds of more modern, postwar, middle-class homes. Up the street, the apple orchard has been cut down and replaced by a Conservative Jewish temple, and over the hilltop is a private school for Hebrew boys and girls. Midway up the hill where the boy dreamt of Nazi storm trooper motorcyclists roaring down at him, the once fiery meeting grounds of German Bundsmen have been miraculously transformed into a summer camp where children of all races and religions splash in pools, strike white baseballs across green lawns, weave clever wicker baskets, and link their arms in communal songfests around evening campfires. And what of all that dark and evil energy? Where did it go? All smoothed over now like the surface of his stone and long forgotten.

Memory soars across time and the globe that they traveled together for over thirty years of enlightenment, hope, and some disillusion before his wife was stricken. They saw a Europe rebuilding but unable still to hide the scars of war; they walked across battlefields and beaches where so many soldiers courageously fought to the death, and they visited concentration camps where so many Jews were slaughtered. The best of the survivors seem able to return and forgive a cleansed German majority and their children—far more perhaps than those like the boy who viewed the horror from afar. Not fixated on war, they feel immortal when traveling across thousands of years of civilization trying to envision and capture the richness of human lives and spiritual moments—from Christ's path to the cross, to the Temple Mount, from Medieval churches, castles and battlefields to the graveyards of saints and everyman and once peering down into a cliffside cave where the Dead Sea Scrolls were discovered. The ancient past of Western civilization lay before them, often in ruins, in aggregations of stones, altars, and edifices requiring a depth of knowledge and imaginative vision to unlock their hidden secrets as the two of them learned to walk among and read the ancient stones.

He places stones, not flowers, upon her gravesite—a signal that he's been there to visit and honor his soul mate. The Hebrew custom of placing stones appeals to Joseph. Not that wind or rain may lack the power to blow these sturdy tributes away but in tune with the image of rock gatherers since ancient times creating altars to their unfathomable Creator. The smallest set of stones carefully placed atop her monument creates an altar to the memory of his beauteous wife. His fingers trace out her name cut deeply into the granite. While her soul may be elsewhere, her monument is a beit olam—a permanent house to which her spirit may safely return. His altar of stones may help contain her restlessness or terror in the face of infinite darkness. Let her spirit remain at rest and find acceptance, if not peace, in the grave and beyond until the time when his spirit seeks to rejoin her. He prays only that she be there for him too in worlds to come—the soul mate he came to trust in this life and who he believes will never betray him in whatever life exists beyond. Tho' powerless still, Joseph traces her name in the stone and feels the comfort of its enduring warmth.

The End

TIME CHORDS
DROWNING

1

Joseph wakes from his dream in the nick of time. He's been soaring across a brilliant green countryside, gliding like a hawk in the uplifting ocean breezes toward a distant, snow-covered peak when his magical rocket pack sputters out, and his body tumbles through space, about to crash headlong into the jagged rocks and oversized boulders of the apple orchard below. When, thank God, a rush of sunlight breaks through his bedroom window dazzling his half-closed eyes with a basketful of warm wall colors. Joseph awakens with a giddy sensation. For the first time he's dreamt of actually flying through the clouds high above earth, feeling new muscular power in his chubby young body, as if transformed from a larval-caterpillar state into a spectacular, colorful butterfly, a breakthrough dream sure to be an omen of good days ahead, and so very different from his two recurring nightmares. The first, a dark watery dream in which his body is sucked down into an enormous black hole beneath the sea where he discovers himself on hands and knees, crawling deep inside a stalactite cave drawn toward an awful odor—that of a half-blind family of Grendel-like monsters hiding in their lair. Sensing human blood, they spring up and claw out at the flesh of their intruder just as he awakens. Joseph's second recurring nightmare is as bad or worse. He stands powerless as a band of Nazi motorcyclists in black glasses race down the mountain road at breakneck speed toward him; unable to move, *his boots stuck in macadam turned to cement, he feels like an insect caught in a web, and there is absolutely no way to escape his certain destruction. But thank God, he always manages to awaken a nanosecond before the brutal force of the onrushing Nazi motorcyclists drive into his body and crush him.*

"Dreams of death, of vanishing, are natural for boys your age," his mother said to comfort him when he told her why he'd cried out one night and run to her bed. "A boy's Illusion that life is everlasting meets up with harsh reality, especially now with war and so many killed each day. None of us will live forever. I won't, you won't. But for boys like you, that reality is decades away so you'd be foolish to anguish over it each day or, as a writer once said, you'll live to die a thousand deaths."

Two years into World War II, Joseph lives with nightmare visions of the Nazis as supermen and their blitzkrieg war machine as unstoppable. His deep fears of Nazi killers are fed by his friend, Peter, who'd been thrown out of school, forced to wear a Jewish Star of David, and beaten by Hitler youth when he ventured out into the Berlin streets.

Peter's parents, German doctor-researchers, were lucky to have family and professional colleagues in America. While Peter lives miles away, they play together once or twice a month now, and his stories of Berlin life are so vivid that Joseph can truly envision the Nazi SS and can feel their brutality in the air around him. He's come to live with dark images of Nazi armies advancing across their countryside, out to kill everyone in sight with hatred and joy, especially if you happened to be born a Jew. So here in America, thousands of miles from the battlefields of Europe, Joseph lives with Peter's heightened fears and evil images; his own mind is consumed with the War. He thinks of little else.

The War is touching most Americans now. His aunt Molla, the army nurse with the first American troops in Morocco, was likely shipped to Sicily; her fiancé, David, a Captain and surgeon is still in England; and the boy's overaged ROTC uncle, Jacob, is awaiting his call to duty. Even Grandfather has signed on as an air-raid warden, and the boy helps. He's learned to identify allied and enemy aircraft from the charts, and he runs up and down the road to neighboring homes and farms during infrequent air-raid drills to check that no lights are showing and report anyone without black shades on all their windows. "With no lights showing," he's told, "enemy aircraft won't waste their bombs on a small country village like ours."

Overseas, America and British allies are becoming victorious. They outflanked and outgunned General Rommel in Tunisian tank battles with the Desert Fox—where his aunt Molla served—and they've chased the Nazis across the Mediterranean, invading the island of Sicily off the coast of Italy. His aunt is likely nursing wounded American soldiers in Sicily now, and they say nightly prayers for her safety. Wartime battles are increasingly brutal, fighting against the self-proclaimed invincible Nazi armies. And it might be worse on Pacific islands like Guadalcanal, where our toughest Marines must use flamethrowers to firebomb the fanatic, fight-to-the-death Jap soldiers out of their steel-and-earth bunkers, burning their bodies crisp to ashes beyond all recognition, which is a most unbelievable, nightmarish image for the boy. In these high-tension wartime afternoons, Joseph and his grandfather read the newspapers together. They watched with growing hopefulness last year when the black-ink arrows with swastikas inside were turned back at the gates of Stalingrad. Britain's bulldog, Prime Minister Winston Churchill, called it the end of the beginning. But neither the boy nor his classmates feel any safer; they've been warned to prepare for a long, bloody war of advances and retreats, told to keep the faith but expect the worst to come. Tens of thousands of American soldiers will be killed and wounded this year, the newspapers say, and no one can predict when this world war might end. President Franklin Delano Roosevelt has demanded unconditional surrender, and neither Hitler, a wild-eyed, would-be-superman, nor the half-god, half-man Japanese Emperor, Hirohito, seems like a leader who'll ever surrender. Older boys claim that these two crazy Satans made a vow in blood to bring the whole world down with them rather than lose the war, an event they call *apocalyptic* that is prophesied in the Bible's Old and New Testaments. Grandfather's newspapers are now talking optimistically about the start of a second front in Europe later this year or next. Invasion of the continent may become the biggest battle of all with thousands of brave soldiers and marines killed or drowned along the beaches of France. Nazi propaganda chief Goebbels warns that their full force will be waiting to destroy us with heavy airpower, panzer tanks, their most vicious SS troops, and miles of massive camouflaged fortifications. The second front invasion will most likely begin after Sicily and the Italian campaign are won, so we must prepare ourselves for one of the deadliest battles in world history.

Nazis believe that winning is all about willpower. *They claim to have the will of supermen and claim that all the rest of us are soft and lack willpower. Peter's ironic but disturbing anti-Nazi song, "Ve ist der master race!" rings out its prophetic warning. Are we Americans too soft? Can we match the Nazis in willpower? Joseph thinks back to his own sandpit fights and stoning by his classmates over two years before; he knows that he has a lot to prove about his own willpower and courage.*

Yet waking this quiet midsummer morning, with school on vacation, half a world apart from the conflict, the boy sinks back on his damp sheets warmed by the early rays of sunlight, and he tries to blank his young mind of all threatening wartime thoughts. Instead, he listens to the early morning songbirds singing out to their families, friends, and lovers. He listens to the two willful roosters in Grandfather's chicken coops out back, crowing loudly and bossing their brood of hens to wake up and start laying eggs. It's not easy for Joseph to blot out the war, but he tricks his mind into forgetfulness by remembering the odor of thick crabgrass that he'd hand mowed yesterday afternoon in their small backyard lawn. Few foods, not even chocolate cake or homemade breads, have a more fragrant odor than freshly cut grass. The boy is always picking sprigs of tasty green weeds to chew on although his classmates often mock him, say he looks like a real country hick. Not that he minds. Far in the distance, Joseph hears a series of comforting whistles as the early morning milk train chugs its way south behind High Tor Mountain, rolling along the east bank of the Hudson River toward the great harbor city of New York. Joseph tries to hold onto these fleeting moments of early morning tranquility by imagining that the war is ended, and he can lie in bed as long as he likes without anxiety about the Nazis invading. Some of his schoolmates ridicule the idea of Heaven as too perfect a place with nothing much to do. But if Heaven exists, Joseph feels sure that he can learn to live there with all its so-called quietude and never-ending peace. No problem at all.

Noises begin to echo throughout the small five-room bungalow as his family starts to awaken, dashing Joseph's moment of heavenly peace. He hears his two-year-old sister through the thin wall, rolling about and starting to whimper. Any minute now she'll wake his nine-month-old baby brother, and Mother and the whole household will spring aggressively to life.

Joseph must move quickly. He tosses off the wet, sweaty sheets and throws on his rumpled shorts, T-shirt and sneakers, leaving his shoelaces untied. It's urgent to make a getaway before Mother wakes and enlists him in her feminine agenda—helping with breakfast, washing dishes, making beds, vacuuming floors, and a list of equally obnoxious household cleaning chores that make her mothering job easier but take hours to complete. And they're not the kind of tasks a ten-year-old boy should be forced to do, not now in wartime, when his real job is to get himself trained and ready to fight the fierce Hitler youth or the small fanatic Japanese soldiers. But his mother thinks logic is on her side, that she holds the trump card. "We give you a room, clothes, and feed you. Nothing's free. Everyone's got to do their part. You can't grow up to be a parasite, a bloodsucker who feeds off everyone else's work." She knows that the bloodsucker part gets to him. Suddenly, the baby begins to cry, and shivers work their way down Joseph's spine as he hears Mother's scratchy morning voice at the crib comforting the child. Only a matter of minutes before she'll come barging into his bedroom, yank the covers off his bed, and order Joseph to pitch in on breakfast or one of her girlie chores. Even summer school would be better, he swears, except for the dishonor of failing a grade. He's got to evacuate like Dunkirk before she busts in and grabs him for the morning.

Great to be invisible like the Shadow, who clouds men's minds so they cannot see him; he'd duck past her skirt and be out the screen door into the bright, sunny yard before she knew it. In war, invisibility could be a great weapon. An invisible man might crawl from tree to tree and disappear across a battlefield unharmed by Nazi gunners. An invisible soldier might walk right past Hitler youth then shoot them in the back of their heads. He might even sneak into Germany to assassinate Hitler and maybe end the War. That might not be far-fetched, for there are many invisible forces walking about, he's sure. "When we die, our spirit leaves our bodies, but many linger here on earth as ghosts," gaptooth Thomas swears. "Especially if you die a horrible death by fire or water or by some other gruesome act. We're surrounded by invisible dead spirits who might rise up and play a big role at a crisis time in your life, a secret your teachers will never tell you." Which is okay with Joseph. One day, he hopes to be lucky enough to meet up with a ghostly spirit and have a new dimension of life or death revealed. No, he's not afraid of the invisible spirit world; he would welcome all spirits and be thrilled to learn the secrets of the dead.

Joseph pushes open the screen and slides his body out of the bedroom window silently, like the well-trained Army Commando he is focused on becoming. He jumps down into a mound of mucky earth surrounding the septic tank and gets a whiff of outhouse odors from their septic hole left partly uncovered. Father and Grandfather built the little white bungalow across from the main farmhouse, but they bungled the septic tank field and spend a few weekends each year opening and closing it with shovels and picks, forever making it wider and deeper, already encroaching so far into the dirt driveway that only one or two visitor cars can park there. Every few months, Father can be found outside, shoulder-deep in the septic hole with a shovel and pick, cursing the rocky, hard-to-absorb constitution of the county's earth. Appropriately enough, *shit* and *crap* are his father's favorite curse words. And for some odd reason, Father chooses to do manual labor in his old business suits; cars often slow or stop along the road to glimpse this eccentric professional man with a white dress shirt and bow tie sinking deeper into his septic hole while shoveling away and mouthing his favorite curse words. Septic systems are a man's job, victory gardens are another, but his inventive father has placed tar paper between tomato plants and the lettuce, eliminating any need for weeding. So Joseph accepts the idea of spending sweaty days ahead in the septic hole; it's far more acceptable than being forced into

Mother's unmanly household tasks. He'll be content to labor with shovel and pick in the hope that his undersized arm and shoulder muscles will begin to grow larger and stronger.

Quicktime required! To meet Joseph's battlefield training agenda, he has no time to waste. Seconds before Mother breaks into his bedroom, he has climbed up the side trellis onto their steeply pitched roof, being light enough still not to pull the trellis down. Crouching on all fours, he edges his body up the shingles and rises to full height behind the brick chimney, where he can survey the countryside. No one in sight early this morning. The cornfields are still empty of the truckloads of pickers brought over by Cropsey, the farmer who rents Grandfather's fields. His pickers are mostly groups of Gypsies, Latinos, a few Negroes, and immigrants, some wearing the filthy clothes they'd slept in and smelling as bad as the septic tank. Pickers are different from the groups of hungry Depression road people, who have mostly disappeared since the start of war. Some pickers are bad hombres and have to be closely watched or they sneak away to steal Grandfather's chickens and eggs from the coops out back. The real world looks to be a dangerous place when it comes to earning a living or just holding onto your property and possessions when so many others have little or nothing and walk the roads hungry. "We can't blame them if their children are starving," Grandfather says, but the old man is looked upon as too damn liberal, a real softy, who goes after the thieves with his fierce, undersized spitz and shoots shotgun blasts into the air to scare but never aims to harm them. He does shoot to kill hawks, though, or red foxes or that intelligent, almost-human acting bobcat that's been menacing their neighborhood farms for months.

The only time Grandfather might have shot to kill a human was just before the war when the Bundsmen marched up their road with American and German flags, drunk with power and singing rally chants on their way up to Davies meeting grounds to burn crosses and curse Jews. When the marchers stopped out front that night and smashed their mailbox, Joseph feared the loud-chanting Bundsmen might storm into the farmhouse and attack them. As the only Jews living on this stretch of road, Cropsey had warned Grandfather to prepare for trouble. The boy will never forget those frightening moments sitting on the stairway behind a sweating Grandfather with his shotgun cocked, but luckily, the Bundsmen decided to move on; and they marched away chanting their songs in that guttural, intimidating manner as if inviting trouble. But all that's changed now with the war on. German-Americans have rallied around the American flag and many have joined the Army to fight the Nazis and prove their loyalty. If they hadn't, old gaptooth Thomas said, President Roosevelt might've rounded them up in detention camps like he did with many US-born Japanese in California for fear of them planting bombs or other anti-American terrorism. "We're all working together now for a common cause," his friend Peter is fond of saying, "to beat all that crazy evil out of the Nazis and Japs, and win freedom and justice for all people no matter how small or weak or different than the so-called Nazi supermen!"

The summer sun is stronger, and its warmth feels good to Joseph, high at his guard post behind the redbrick chimney watchtower, seeing no enemies in sight. He's escaped the early morning reach of his demanding, Grendel-like mother, but stealth is required even high on the bungalow roof. If she hears the sound of his body sliding down the shingles, she'll be out on the lawn in a flash, screaming for him to get right down and help her. Help is the real issue, although Mother claims it frightens her, brings pangs to her heart when she sees him walking high atop the roof, fearing he might fall off and seriously hurt himself. A decade before, her cousin—a bull of a young man—stepped into an empty elevator shaft when its doors misfired, opening wide, and he'd fallen five floors to his death. Since then, Mother developed an extreme fear of heights. That very sense of danger pleases young Joseph as he tiptoes across the peak of the steep roof, trying to keep his body in perfect balance like American Indian skyscraper workers—an act that "scared her to death" when she watched him perform it a few weeks ago. Afterward, she kept him in the house all day doing girls' work as punishment. A good reason to exit the roof quickly now. So Joseph slides noiselessly down the green shingles to the roof's back edge eight feet above the grass strip; he imagines himself as a paratrooper about to jump down into enemy territory, pulling his rip cord thousands of feet in the sky. Joseph hits the ground with a sharp thud and rolls over into the rock wall, holding his breath, hoping that no one's heard him drop. Still all clear inside the house. Not a sound. But Joseph's ankle begins to throb and hurt. It feels as if it might swell. He gets angry at himself. This is just the kind of weakness that might cause your capture or death on a battlefield. The boy decides he will practice fighting pain and steels his mind to ignore the hurt. He rises to his feet, springs across the rock wall, and enters the tall, ripe, still mostly unpicked cornfield on the rolling hillside, bending low as he runs. All the enemy might see exposed is the top of a dark head bobbing above the corn as Joseph darts right and left through the tall cornstalks to create his invisible Commando escape from the guns of large Nazi tanks that he imagines he hears grinding their way down the steep country road.

Having escaped the Nazi tanks, Joseph imagines himself a football halfback like the great Red Grange, cutting sharply and stopping on a dime, his youthful shoulders gliding between hundreds of hapless cornstalk tacklers, taking care to smash down and destroy as few as possible until he runs out of breath and dives down into the rich red soil on the far side of Grandfather's six-acre cornfield. Sports are exciting.

They can capture your imagination and can be real helpful in physical training, but sports are not serious enough to believe in during wartime. A fancy-stepping halfback like Red Grange would be shot to pieces if he tried to dodge across a cornfield and attack a real Nazi machine gun nest. On a battlefield, Joseph knows he will have to learn to sweat out the little things, to crawl one foot at a time or maybe dig in and lie there silently, passively for hours or even days, fighting his own body's needs, ignoring hunger, pain and keeping one eye open, alert and awake through the darkest night so the enemy can't sneak up on their platoon. It's these patient, wormlike actions, older boys say, that keep real soldiers alive in the middle of firefights, and they are the hardest actions to practice. Joseph does practice holding his breath underwater in the bathtub to increase his lung power, and he counts the seconds up to a minute thirty-three so far. It seems impossible that he'll get anywhere near the two-minute mark, but he keeps trying even when water goes down the wrong pipe and he finds himself choking. Another challenging test is to sneak up into the windowless attic on the hottest days of summer and do push-ups and sit-ups while fighting off the relentless noonday heat under the shingled roof. But the boy's favorite maneuver is practicing stealth, moving quietly from tree to tree and target shooting along the way. Sniping at enemy soldiers is not like hunting deer from a blind since humans are much more cunning, the most dangerous animal of all. Joseph practices peripheral vision, looking in all directions at once for signs of near-invisible Nazi snipers who could be watching his platoon from what may appear to be an empty attic window or a church steeple, waiting to surprise them and shoot down at the back of their exposed heads. One mistake of not being watchful or not "living fully in the moment" like a Buddhist priest does and *whack* you're dead in wartime.

Joseph learned to shoot a .22-caliber rifle at the tender age of five, taught by his uncle who'd enlisted in ROTC at Cornell. Uncle Jacob nailed a colorful red-and-white target to the trunk of a giant oak tree in his own backyard early one morning and ordered the boy to hold the rifle steady, press the trigger, and hit the center bull's-eye. The target tree turned out to be right next to a normally empty little bungalow where two of his aunts happened to be sleeping over that morning, including Molla, the Army nurse now in Sicily. His two aunts woke up in a fury and put a hysterical end to his ROTC uncle's target practice. "Letting that little boy shoot a gun is crazy enough, but he could have missed the tree and killed us both!" His uncle laughed and began to sing his favorite ROTC war song, "Famous Roger Young." But Uncle Jacob made sure the bungalow was empty when they resumed target practice, and the boy learned to shoot a real .22 rifle and hit part of the target most of the time. "We've got to learn to protect ourselves. Most people don't have a clue," his uncle explained. "Don't expect others to protect you if we ever should go to war. You're never too young to learn." Joseph didn't tell his father about the .22 rifle target practice with Uncle Jacob for fear he'd put a stop to it. Like most of his classmates, the boy target practices with his BB gun alone in the woods. While his parents bought him the BB gun, they have no idea how often he uses it, buying box after box of BBs in the community market with his lunch money. Joseph keeps his BB gun and ammunition hidden under a canvas among broken car parts in their former cowshed. He makes his way to the shed now, crouching and zigzagging back across the cornfield, ignoring the pain from his ankle, which has begun to swell.

Grandfather surprised everyone by getting a job as a part-time night watchman at the nearby Army embarkation camp, where he is required to carry a loaded pistol. Troopships on return trips from the European theater are expected to bring a few Nazi and Italian POWs back to the US and hold them temporarily in the camp. Joseph looks expectantly at Grandfather every night to learn whether any Nazi prisoners have arrived yet and, if so, if any have tried to escape. Will the old man act heroically, he wonders, or will he let Nazi prisoners escape rather than shoot his pistol to stop them? And what will the camp commander do to the old man if he holds his fire and lets a Nazi prisoner escape—fire him from work or place him in an Army detention prison for aiding the enemy? Joseph isn't surprised when Grandfather empties his pockets and places his bullets in a neat row on the kitchen table, looking like toy soldiers beside his unloaded revolver and holster. Joseph is ashamed of his grandfather's softness in the face of Nazi brutality to Jews and to all American GIs; he prays that a Nazi POW won't escape into the woods on Grandfather's watch and scare all the schoolkids and neighbors. If a Nazi POW does escape, the boy will volunteer to join the search, for hardly anyone knows the woods behind their farm as well as Joseph. He's pencil drawn crude but detailed maps of the trees, rocks, and bushes, studied the secret places where someone might hide over a two-mile or so radius in their backwoods. There are some pretty neat hiding places for an escapee or for any US resistance fighter, including himself, if the Nazis ever do invade America and set out to capture their small village because it houses the county courthouse and prison.

Joseph retrieves his BB gun from under the moldy canvas in the cowshed then makes his way past the chicken coops and outdoor latrines into the forest without anyone seeing him—neither gaptooth Thomas, who's away at one of his church meetings, nor the bent figure of his grandmother carrying pails of water back to the chickens. The boy practices moving with stealth from tree to tree like an Indian, careful not to step on twigs or piles of leaves, making his way to a large fallen oak tree hit by lightning, under which he'd dug out a cave. It is well hidden in a heavily vined thicket behind a mound of rocks and earth formed by the uprooted, hollowed-out trunk. The cave itself is still too small; he must bring Father's pick and shovel into the woods to get it to a size where he can sit upright out of sight. This is the place where he might survive for weeks or months if he learns enough about natural foods, like roots and nuts, mushrooms and berries. But he will need a deeper cave to live in, and he'll need to buy or steal a real gun, more like his uncle's .22-caliber rifle rather than his grandfather's limited shotgun.

If the Nazi invade, the boy pictures himself as part of the underground resistance, an almost invisible figure living in the forest, scouting out Nazi encampments, supply routes, and enemy snipers. He'll pass information along to underground leaders, and maybe they'll ask him to join them. Training for that event, the boy practices shooting his BB gun nearly every day, aiming at trunks of large trees, smaller saplings, or individual clusters of leaves, some hanging down in ways that resemble soldier's heads or shoulders and backs. Last fall, he made three pumpkin jack-o'-lanterns and shot them to bits. The chief objective is surprise; next is precision in hitting your target with the first shot so you can race off before the enemy can guess the direction of the shooter. Recently, he'd begun to practice quick shooting in series like Sergeant York, the famous hillbilly sharpshooter in the movie that he and his friends had seen about World War I trench warfare. The Germans never knew what hit them or that all the killing came from a single soldier, not a whole platoon. When he captured nearly a hundred German soldiers and led them to American lines, the Germans must have thought he was like a herd dog, but there had to be twenty or thirty American soldiers behind him hidden from sight; otherwise, they'd never have surrendered to a single soldier no matter how murderously good he was with a rifle. But it will be much harder to surprise

*the Nazis in this war with their tanks and armored vehicles along with far
better communications devices and the ability to call in airpower.*

Hearing a sudden sharp sound, Joseph hurls his body to the ground
behind a cluster of thick bushes. He lies there silently then spots a rabbit
scurrying off. Last hunting season, he'd actually been fired at once, but
he jumped out of the bushes and screamed at the two red-faced old
hunters, who'd stopped in their tracks. They didn't apologize for the shot.
Instead they cursed and warned him to "stay the hell out of their woods
this time of year." As if the woods and forests belonged to hunters and
no one else dare enter during hunting season—a sentiment that his father
agreed with, angry at the boy for playing war games and tempting fate.

Safe inside his secret cave, Joseph begins to feel hunger pains, and
his ankle is constantly throbbing. Almost time to go home for breakfast
and face Mother and her chores; he'd return later to pick natural foods
and plan more Army maneuvers. Besides, it's slowly becoming a hot,
steamy morning. There'll be a blazing sun by noon. He'll stop along the
way home to use the heavily limed outhouse located behind the long,
four-section chicken coop next to one of the three single-room chicken
coops that his grandparents lived in last summer when renting the
main farmhouse to city folks. It was tough for them with no electricity,
using kerosene lamps and a makeshift stove, no running water, and
the smelly outhouse, but that's how most people lived for thousands of
years. It was just as raw as gaptooth Thomas's one-room former coop
that he comes and goes from while doing handyman work on the farm
in exchange for rent and meals. But early this spring, Grandfather built
a small apartment above the converted barn for himself and Grandma
with all the modern basics we take for granted: a toilet, running water,
electricity, and gas. Downstairs is the apartment he'd converted a decade

ago for his dying mother that he rents out summers to the Socolows and Caplans—two older intellectual couples without children, who come up from the city on Fridays through Sunday, and pay little rent for their weekends on the farm.

The main farmhouse rental is Grandfather's chief source of summer income. This year he rented it to a supposedly wealthy rabbi and his family who'd managed to escape from Austria or Hungary five or six years after the Nazis came to power in Germany. They have two sons: Shlomo, who is three years older, and Danny, a half year younger than Joseph. "Our boy will have friends his own age this summer," Grandfather said hopefully. But alas, the rabbi's two boys, Shlomo and Danny, are content to keep their own company, which includes daily study of the Talmud, vigorous shouting matches about dumb things, arguing about politics, such as the merits of Zionism, or huddling together over a chessboard on the farmhouse porch. They seldom talk of Europe and, unlike Peter, never speak about Nazis or the war. Sometimes, young Danny emerges from the brotherly cocoon and begs Joseph to play catch with a baseball. He fancies himself a pitcher with what he calls his special inside-out screwball, like Carl Hubbell of the Giants, but his pitch is slower than a knuckleball, and it looks pretty easy to hit if you really wanted to. Otherwise, speaking Yiddish or German and stopping every afternoon to pray with yarmulkes and tefillin, they keep aloof from Joseph. Even when he goes up onto the porch to watch them play chess, they never offer him a game. Joseph's father taught him to play chess, and the boy thinks he might be as good or better than young Danny, but he never challenges them, and they never ask. Worst of all, his neighborhood friend Dougie has stopped coming over to play catch or war games; he's disappeared since the Jewish family took over the farmhouse. When Joseph met a classmate at the community market, Kenny laughed and teased him about the "Yid farmers." Had the Europeans bought his grandfather's farm? And do the rabbi's sons make Joseph wear a skullcap and pray with them twice a day?

The boy feels embarrassed. He has a hard time admitting the great distance he feels between these two European Jewish boys and himself. Part of it is due to Joseph's mother, who is from a Russian background and typically mocks organized religion. She doesn't keep a kosher home, never lights candles on the Sabbath, skips going to temple, and spends no time at all praying or reading the Bible or Talmud, choosing instead an array of modern novelists, like Dorothy Parker and Lillian Hellman. Mother thinks of herself as a distinctly emancipated American woman. She'd played forward on the first women's high school championship basketball team in the county, and she had her girlfriends over for book-club discussions or to giggle together and flapper dance the Charleston to the latest recordings—that is, before having her two babies. The conservative farmhouse renters, although civil, avoid contact with Mother; on the other hand, they seem genuinely fond of Grandfather, especially his helpfulness at all hours of the day or night when the plumbing or lights need fixing or when they got a flat tire or when they don't understand how to tune the old crystal-set radio. It was a far different story with the Soccies and Cappies, who come from Greenwich Village. They are avid readers and crossword- puzzle solvers, and they bring a never-ending supply of the latest jokes and gossip and are thought of as almost part of the family. They too seem to have less in common with the orthodox farmhouse Europeans, although the heavyset rabbi waddles out back to sit and chat with them on weekends while his wife is busy in the kitchen cooking up his favorite Sabbath feasts.

It was weird, thought Joseph, how Grandfather's farm turns into a convergence of so many worlds during the summertime, with religious, kosher, Jewish refugees dominating the farmhouse in front, Greenwich Village intellectuals out back, reading on lawn chairs, and his displaced grandparents living in the converted barn's new upstairs apartment. While below, there's a hot incubator room with the chirping of emerging chicks. Not to mention old gaptooth Thomas in his one-room coop out back, his life devoted to Jesus, wandering off between East and West Coasts in winters. And periodically, the small army of pickers dumped by Cropsey's truck into the fields at dawn to pick the corn and beans when ripe for harvest. Outside this international conclave is his friend Dougie and Joseph's classmates in town, keeping their distance from the Yid farm. Ten miles south is the Army embarkation camp where Grandfather works part-time, loaded pistol or not, and well beyond America's shores, heavily armed soldiers and terrified civilians engage in the most destructive world war in history—with his mother's sister, Molla, nursing the wounded in Sicily. While back in Russia, his grandmother Bubby's native land, the Nazi army was turned back at Stalingrad and are retreating; in the Pacific, the decisive naval battle of Midway was won, and fierce fighting with Japanese soldiers moved from Guadalcanal to other islands, and the boy's favorite General, Douglas MacArthur, has vowed to return to the Philippines.

On that peaceful summer morning, Joseph sits in the quiet of his small cave, listening for any intrusion, any new, distinct sound other than the flight of birds or scurry of small animals through the leaves. In wartime, sounds of conflict might break through at any moment and shatter time. He must be on guard in this time of wide-scale slaughter, where the angel of death may be anywhere, springing out from behind the most seemingly peaceful bushes or trees. Joseph crawls to the edge of his cave with his BB gun held tight against his shoulder and props it against a rock to steady his firing. He is practicing the art of listening and patiently waiting, ready for whatever form of evil may be approaching;

he imagines he sees shadows, a group of tall hunters entering the forest about to shred the eerie silence. Joseph's father thinks Peter's Nazi stories have led to craziness, a ridiculous obsession with a far-off war that he is too young to ever have to fight. Well, so far his father is right. He focuses on last night's wonderful dream of soaring through space above the brilliant green countryside. With all the sounds of a benign forest around him, the boy falls into a pleasant half doze, half sleep.

Joseph jolts himself awake, angry that he's dozed off at his post, which is dereliction of duty for a real soldier, an action that could put him in the guardhouse for endangering his entire squad. Concentration is by far the hardest part of training to be a soldier. He must learn to concentrate harder if he ever expects to beat the Hitler youth, who may be older and stronger and have more battlefield experience. But it's midmorning already, and feeling starved, the boy decides it's time to start home.

On the way, Joseph enters gaptooth Thomas's empty cabin to avoid running into Grandma on her hourly trips to the chicken coops, balancing two pails of water below her sloping shoulders. Thomas is away, off to one of his Christian meetings in the Amish hills of Pennsylvania. His cabin is stark—a chair, a table, a bed, and a small kerosene stove; there is no running water or inside toilet. Beside the bed, there is an ancient metal candelabra, and pasted on the wall is a huge black-and-white poster reproduction of a Renaissance painting of Jesus Christ on the Cross. Thomas donates a tithe for every dollar he earns without anyone even asking. Grandfather lets him stay in the chicken coop without rent and shares family meals with him in exchange for farmwork, tool sharpening, and carpentry. Joseph enjoys dropping in unexpectedly on gaptooth Thomas, who seldom talks to others but likes preaching his lessons or parables to the boy, who is curious and a good listener. While they are totally different people, Grandfather shows great respect for Thomas and his single-minded devotion to his Christian faith while Thomas speaks of the old man as his Hebrew brother, Abraham, telling the boy that "a life force" brought them together.

Leaving gaptooth Thomas's empty cabin, Joseph makes his way to the incubator hot room, where he enjoys watching tiny chicks emerge from their shells and chirp away at each other. Grandfather is sent cardboard boxes with eggs, which he, and sometimes Joseph, carefully place on the incubator shelves to raise a new home flock of hens each year for egg production or to sell to the bald-headed kosher butcher, who *davens* an ancient, holy Jewish prayer then slits their free-range chickens' throats. It's great fun to watch the young chicks emerge into life and chirp away at each other as long as he keeps their final destination out of mind. Yet chickens are called "dumb birds" raised for food, and Grandfather treats them well, at least up until their final moments in the butcher's thick hands.

Grandfather insists that Joseph go with him to the bald-headed kosher butcher's shop, and the boy tries not to turn his eyes away until after the first hen is killed; then he finds an excuse to step outside. "They're killing all the Jews in Europe! Believe me!" the butcher protests. Few people actually believe him: they think butchers see the world in a different way—from the cutting-knife, underbelly side. As a real soldier, the hardest thing will be to learn to kill the enemy and accept human death, especially the screams and suffering of your wounded Army buddies. It's easy to learn to kill, older boys swear, if you focus on the faces of the Nazi bastards out to kill you. If you visualize killing as self-defense, it becomes so instinctive to strike back that you'll never shed a tear afterward. The killing part will be difficult for him, Joseph knows. He'll have to work at it. Being killed yourself is a strong possibility, but saving others by sacrificing yourself is a hero's act; and maybe it's okay to die knowing you saved the lives of others. Strangely, dying is not the worst Joseph fears. Far worse is getting wounded and left behind on the battlefield in great pain from an explosion or gunshot then being captured by the Nazis and tortured beyond what even the most brave grown-ups can withstand. The boy imagines carpenter nails hammered into his eye sockets or into the soles of his feet, his weakest spot, just like the Greek soldier Achilles. There were unthinkable Nazi tortures that could surely break his spirit and cause him to die the death of a helpless young Jewish coward after all. But a real soldier cannot allow his mind to fantasize on the most terrible death imaginable; he must train himself to simply plug along step-by-step and watch his buddies' backs. Just as it's much more fun to watch the exuberant young chicks at play rather than dwell on their dark futures, it's far better to put the images of Nazi torture out of mind until those future, impossible-to-bear moments force themselves upon you.

Hungry as his stomach feels, he hesitates before crossing the lawn to his front door and having to confront Mother and try to explain his early morning disappearance. Instead, Joseph swings himself up into his favorite cherry tree located between the main farmhouse and the renovated barn. He finds a cluster of ripe cherries on a lower limb, sits and nibbles on them slowly one by one, enjoying their rich taste. He enjoys seeing how far out onto the lawn he can spit the pits. The Socolows and Cappies often tease Joseph for being lazy, avoiding his farm-boy chores, whenever they catch him sitting up in the grand old cherry tree. Not that he minds their teasing; he's content to perch there for a half hour or more, savoring the taste of ripe cherries. And it's located out of Mother's sight line from the bungalow, a place where he can hang out and consider a lot of mixed-up, clashing ideas about growing up that are tough to sort out when the world is at war. His main focus is to grow up more quickly and become self-sufficient, brave enough to survive alone in the woods and maybe join the underground and sabotage the Nazis if they do invade. If so, he's sure to meet other boys like himself in the American underground, like in the undergrounds of France and Poland. Some of the toughest resistance groups, he's heard, won't let a Jew join them, but he feels sure that won't happen in America, where everyone is encouraged to join the teams no matter what your background. All, that is, except Negroes, or the weird Jackson-Whites—who are half-Dutch and half-native-Indian—who live an inbred hermit existence in the nearby Ramapo Mountains.

Joseph encountered a young Jackson-White boy in his woods only once; the white-haired boy with red, bloodshot eyes was lost but not at all frightened. The two boys stood staring at each other in a game of willpower to see who'd blink first. The Jackson-White was very good at it, acting as if he could stand frozen in time forever, and Joseph began to sweat. Then, in an instant, the boy seemed to evaporate into a cluster of saplings, and he was gone as if this child of the forest was able to blend into the trees and become as invisible as the Shadow. Joseph felt envious of the weird boy's gifts. "Part of the rich magic that resides in the forest," old Thomas told him, "that few of us are able to see. You may be one of the lucky ones." Joseph hopes to meet the Jackson-White boy again and win him over so that he and his magic will become an underground teammate of Joseph's rather than an estranged enemy. If the Nazis invade, he will team up and fight alongside everyone and exclude no one, not even girls.

"Hey, Joseph!" Looking down through the tree limbs, Joseph sees two yarmulke heads bobbing about and yelling up at him. The rabbi's sons had been on their farmhouse porch, and seeing Joseph up in the cherry tree, they've run over hollering that they've been looking for him all morning, which was unusual. *They must need me for some good reason.* Then he remembers. When first renting, the boys asked if there were any swimming pools in the neighborhood, and Grandfather spoke of a number of lakes, although they weren't exactly next door. And some were restricted—like the lake Dougie and his family go to—while others were pretty far away or closed for the war. Joseph had gone swimming only once that summer, when mother drove them out to Long Beach on the Atlantic Ocean to visit their cousins, including Johnny, who runs a hot-dog stand on the beach. Today, being one of the hottest days in midsummer, the rabbi's sons must want him to take them swimming. If asked, he promised Grandfather he'd take them the first time; after that, they can go by themselves.

The two heads, with yarmulkes bobbing, yell up at him, "Today's the day to take us to that lake you talked about, okay?" "You promised to take us when the weather got really hot."

"I don't think I can do it today," Joseph protests, jumping down from the cherry tree's lower limb and feeling a jolt of pain as his swollen ankle hits the ground.

"Hey! Your old grandpa promised you'd take us," young Danny yells. "My farmhouse is in the middle of Lake Country, he told the rabbi over the phone, hundreds of lakes in all directions!"

"He'd never say lakes. Bodies of water, maybe, including pools, the Hudson River, and Atlantic Ocean beaches—not just lakes."

"Come on, today's the hottest day of summer," Shlomo pleads. "If you won't take us today, Joseph, we'll never ask you again."

"Even if I felt like going, my mother has work for me. I have to help her with all my chores. She'd never let me go until I finish."

"Go ask her," Shlomo says. "Tell her what your grandpa promised when he pleaded with the rabbi to rent his stupid old farmhouse."

"Okay, I'll ask," Joseph responds. "But I know my own mother. She's real tough. She'll never let me go before I do my chores."

"I'll come along with you," Danny insists, "so she can see it's really to help us and help your grandpa keep his word. He said his word is like 'gold.' Isn't that what he said, Shlomo? Ha!"

Joseph is annoyed when young Danny follows after him. The two boys act like the rent their rabbi father pays is so high that it pays for everyone's services, including his and his family's; they act like big boss's sons entitled to help from all quarters. Oh, swimming might be a good idea with this heat wave, but he didn't want to go with them. He'll feel like a chauffeur. They'll use him to get them there then ignore him and play their own games. When Joseph enters the front door with Danny close behind, Mother surprises him by not pouncing on him immediately and ordering him to start work. She puts the baby down, brushes crumbs off her blouse and slacks, and acts quite pleased to see that Joseph is playing with the rabbi's son. "We're not exactly playing together, Maw," he mumbles. "They want me to take them swimming 'cause it's so hot out today."

"Why that's a marvelous idea," she says without her usual irony or edge. *My god, she wants them to like her,* Joseph thinks, amazed by her reaction. "But is there an adult going with you?" "Yes, Ma'am," Danny chimes in, knowing his brother, Shlomo, was recently bar mitzvahed and made a man according to Jewish law.

"He just means his brother Shlomo's thirteen, Maw," Joseph quickly explains, trying to indicate his feelings by shaking his head. "No, Maw, no grown-up adults will be going with us."

"Do you have permission from your father and mother?"

"Sure. Anytime Joseph offers to take us," Danny says. "Are you certain it's all right with your parents?" she asks, some doubts arising at his all-too-facile answers. "Sure," he says. "I mean, we're just talking about a swim in a dumb old lake to cool off. It's no big deal, Ma'am."

"Both you boys swim?" Mother asks. "Are you good swimmers?"

"Better than him, I bet." Danny laughs, pointing at Joseph. "Our dad took us swimming all the time as kids in the old country. At the lakeshore mostly, but in rivers too, with pretty strong currents."

"Do I have to take them today, Maw, if I really don't really feel like going?" It suddenly occurs to his mother that Joseph is being pushed into something he doesn't necessarily want to do. Then young Danny speaks up in his whiniest voice.

"His grandpa told my father, the rabbi, there are lots of lakes in the neighborhood, and he promised that if we rented, 'the boy' would take us. I mean, just a few hours to get out of the heat wave. What else is there to do out here in farm country?" Danny's attitude comes across with arrogance, putting mother off, yet it might be good for Joseph to have friends his own age, even ones she isn't so crazy about.

"All right, just for a few hours. Is anyone home to drive you?" They both shook their heads. "I suppose it's not that far to walk. You boys won't mind a long walk in all this heat?"

"No problem for us, Ma'am. I'll betcha city boys do twice as much walking as any of you country folks." Danny smiles, seeing how easy it is to win Mother over. "We'll get our bathing trunks. Meet you on our front porch, Joseph." He runs out, slamming the screen door behind him.

"His porch!" Mother says, annoyed at being played by Danny. "You didn't want to go with them, did you?"

"It's all right, I guess," Joseph mumbles. "I promised grandpa."

On the way to his room to find his bathing suit, Joseph stops to gulp down a glass of milk and grab a ripe banana and a buttered roll from the kitchen; that will do for breakfast. Passing the baby's room, he hears constant whining and crying. All things considered, going for a swim even with the rabbi's weird sons, beats staying home and having to clean the house or babysit for his little sister or new baby brother. And he might be lucky to meet some of his schoolmates at the lake; maybe they can have fun, like swimming races or starting a softball game or maybe playing one of their favorite war games. It could be an exciting afternoon at the lake.

Joseph thinks of his dream of flight across the brilliant green valley; dreaming of that first flight is a good omen. But next time he hopes that his rocket backpack won't fail, and he'll be able to glide back down to earth as gracefully as one of Grandfather's troublesome long-tailed hawks.

2

The three boys' journey to the nearby lake in the oppressive heat of the midday sun seems endless to the rabbi's sons. "Hey! Where are you leading us, little Moses, into another state?" Shlomo hollers out, holding his side and breathing hard. "I've got to rest. I can't walk another step in this heat." Both rabbi's sons are wearing heavy black shirts and long black pants and with yarmulkes on their heads, the fierce noonday sun has them swimming in perspiration. In contrast, Joseph is wearing his bathing trunks and a plain white T-shirt, and even he is feeling the heat. He's also begun to hobble a bit now that his ankle has swollen. But their kibitzing is the worst part of the trip for Joseph. Everything is either too hard, too hilly or too far or there are too many mosquitos and bugs or the weed pollen in the air makes it hard to breathe. Philips Lake is the nearest public swimming hole from their farm, three and a half miles away; the first part is a shortcut through the rough, hilly woods before they come out onto a long flat stretch of pavement called Dutchman's Road. Along the way, they pass only a few scattered farmhouses until they approach a hidden cluster of older residential homes surrounding a small lake and hear the lively sounds of boys and girls diving, splashing and screaming in the water.

"Here at last!" yells an exuberant Shlomo, surging ahead.

"No, wait up! We're not allowed in there," Joseph explains. "It's restricted! Mostly Dutch and German families who live around a small lakefront, but they have a real nice diving board, I hear."

"No Jews allowed at all?" asks Shlomo, always concerned about such matters. Joseph shakes his head sadly. "Well, how much farther is it to our lake?" Shlomo asks.

"Not too far. Right up that rise and around the bend." "Are you sure our lake's not restricted too?" "No, it's public, open to everyone, even us." Joseph laughs. "I swam there three or four times last summer. Just a few minutes more and you'll have all the swimming you want." Tired of listening to their complaints, Joseph trots on ahead, anxious to finally deliver them to their watery destination.

Keep Out! A huge handwritten sign with strong red rectangular letters has been painted on a black backboard high above the lake's front gates. Below it, a smaller sign declares, "Closed for Season. Absolutely No Admittance!" Confronting Joseph is a tall wire fence that runs off around the lake in both directions as far as he can see. The fence has a barbed wire section on top angled outward like Army installation fences or the scary concentration camp fences in movie newsreels to prevent illegal prisoners or trespassers any hope of entry or escape. Better to be on the outside and not imprisoned, free to walk away and never look back. Inside the tall wire gates, there is no movement, not a soul in sight. A twin-track dirt roadway runs between high, straggly grass and tall weeds, winding its way past two changing shacks for Men and Women. Joseph remembers them being as crudely built as his grandfather's chicken coops and covered by the same layers of heavy green tarpaper. The driveway curls down past the changing shacks, a slight grade leading to the landlocked man-made lake which is filled to the brim from the recent summer rains. Close by the gate, Joseph watches the fierce midday sunlight bounce off the high blue waters of the lake, creating a bubbling surface that looks like vibrating diamonds. The lake itself looks wonderful, far better than Joseph ever remembers it, doubly enhanced now since it appears they've been shut out and will be unable to swim in its cool sparkling blue waters. Joseph grabs hold of the wire fence and begins to shake it angrily as he waits for Shlomo and Danny to arrive, knowing they'll be furious.

"Closed!" Shlomo repeats. "Closed for the season?" The rabbi's sons react shamelessly in their disgust with Joseph; they plunk their backsides down on towels, crushing the tall weeds to create an animal nesting space between the black macadam road and the wire fence. Shlomo places his bag atop his head to shield him from the bright sunlight. Acting exhausted, sweating badly from the long, hot trek, young Danny begins to chant a steady stream of curses in Yiddish and English, most aimed at Joseph, to express his frustration. "Schmuck! Pretty stupid the schmuck making us walk all the way here, not knowing the freakin' lake's closed for the war." "Stop cursing!" Shlomo says, shoving his brother aside. "Isn't there another lake or public swimming pool nearby?" "Nearest one's up by the Valley, another five or six miles away," Joseph explains. "Pretty far to walk. We'd need to have someone drive us there and back." "Who can drive us? Rabbi's in the City. What about the old man, your grandpa?" "He's working at the Army camp as a guard most afternoons."

"What a wasted day!" Danny shouts, throwing a rock across the empty road. "What a complete schnook! Got no idea what's going on in his own village, his own backyard. A country putz, what can you expect?"

"Quiet, you're not helping anyone," says Shlomo.

"What're we gonna do now?" Danny whines, "Just turn our asses around and walk all the way home on the hottest day all summer. Hey, where do you think you're going?" he yells as a disgusted Joseph wanders off across the road and away from the closed front gate.

Plucking a long green stem from its weedy scabbard along the road, Joseph circles back to them, chewing rapidly on the stem. "I told you guys I didn't care about going swimming today," he shouts at them. "Anyway, we can hike back home by a shortcut through the woods. There's a secret bear cave I can show you next to a waterfall that washes over colored rocks. A hidden place no one knows about." The rabbi's sons aren't interested in colored rocks or secret places or any water other than the kind they can plunge into and splash on each other. They sprawl out in the high grass ten yards from the gate, huddling together and ducking down out of sight when a rare car drives by every five or ten minutes. It is early afternoon and the sun is burning down on them in increasing waves of heat.

"Hey, putz! I thought you're practicing to be a hotshot Army Commando," Danny mocks him. "A real Commando would find a way in. He'd find a hole in the fence, or a limb to climb over." "That's not a good idea," his older brother warns. "Why not?" "Because it's illegal. We could get into a lot of trouble." "What trouble?" Danny insists. "Who would know we were ever here?"

Joseph flees from their agitated company and walks over to the far side of the gate, which is angled slightly out of kilter and looks rusted. The sun's rays are very hot now, settling on the back of his neck, and he begins to feel a bit dizzy from the heat. Inside the fence, Philips Lake stretches out and begins to sparkle, taking on the ever-pulsating image of diamonds. Outside looking in, Joseph's own frustration builds: a moment of stillness in which the lake slowly becomes the center of his universe, the single most desirable object on earth. True, Joseph hasn't allowed himself to think too much about swimming this summer. But now that he has come all this way, the thought of fine, cool water works on his senses. His nose pressed against the hot wire gate, he feels the exquisite beauty of his naked body diving down, away from the blistering sun and into the cool waters of the diamond-like lake. He imagines splashing his way out to the raft then letting his body sink deeper into its depths until his stomach scrapes along the cool therapeutic mud along the lake's bottom. This image of gliding along the cool lake persists. For his own bodily relief as well as theirs, Joseph feels he must find a way into this most desirable lake in spite of all the illegal warnings.

Danny the pain, got it right for once. An Army Commando would never let a fence stop him, even if it meant illegal entry and risk of getting into trouble with the military police. Who would it harm if they broke into the lake for a few minutes, took a quick dip, and were gone in a flash? Danny's right—no one would ever know they'd been here. Like gaptooth Thomas's riddle, is the noise of a tree falling in an empty forest truly noise if no one's there to hear it? His mind made up, the boy puts on his grim commando face while the barbed wire fence and locked gate take on the face of the enemy.

He's never liked fences anyway. Fences are built to keep people like him and his family out—out of private pools, gated communities, country clubs for the rich, private schools with their tony air of privilege, global corporations in huge skyscrapers who hire the least number of Jews by quota systems, and all kinds of fancy events, like church and community parties hidden behind high shrubbery and expensive steel fencing where he and his family were neither invited nor desired. These strong feelings of exclusion have been in the air around him since Joseph was a toddler and listened to the fascinating stories of his Russian-born

Bubby Sarah, who has a round peasant's face and a flair for open political rebellion.

"In old country, he yell at us go way, not press you big fat noses on our windows. In America, okay we look in windows. He builds glass walls, glass doors that open into fancy rooms and invite us in. 'Walk in,' he say, 'come meet all people like us and different.' We listen to each other. We can do business together in America because people listen to each other. Constitution says, 'We are the people.' Here, we are the people and our vote counts. One woman, one vote. I count as much as any man!" He listens to her endless fairy tales in which the poor triumph. They never fail. But when in a bad mood, she tells him about the horrible pogroms at the turn of the century in and around Kishinev, Bessarabia, when Cossacks, criminals, and mostly ordinary Russki peasants went berserk, galloping their horses through the shtetl, whipping them, stealing their money, burning their homes, carrying young girls off into the woods for lovemaking, and once killing a brave young rabbi who tried to stop them. None are safe during pogroms, not even the strongest men. And if you're a young girl, pretty or not, there's no place you can hide. She'd been twelve the first time, nearly fifteen the second time they came, and she showed the boy how she fought off one of the men with a garden rake. "America's a long distance from pogroms." She laughs her brightest laugh. They'd left a money-making mill and their possessions in dark of night. Few realized till next day that they were gone. They sneaked across borders, bribed police and border guards, but bribing is dangerous and one time it backfired. They got arrested but talked their way out. "The first to leave are bravest but cold in our hearts too," she said. "We leave our old sick mothers, old aunts, promised we'd send for them, promises we don't keep." On their journey, they faced border fences too and searched for vulnerable places to slip through and fool or pay off the armed border guards. They learned humiliating tricks as well—how to make themselves "small,"

nearly invisible when passing through some towns, blending into crowds of strangers, alien populations where "you dasn't speak or risk giving all of us away." She kept focused on America, hid money in her corset and other secret places for a prized ship's passage to a real paradise where there are no pogrom slaughters encouraged by authorities. "Here in America, we have rights. Bill of Rights say we the people!" she laughed. He loved to hear her laugh the last laughs. No, Bubby Sarah would have never let a wire fence or a No Trespassing sign stop her on her journey, even if it was illegal to break in and enter a forbidden place. She'd find a way to break through, and all of them would sit around and laugh about it afterward.

Intense and up close, studying the angled front gate, Joseph notices that the far side of the gate by the rusted lock looks fragile. He begins to shake it back and forth and feels a strange, weakening sensation. What would a real Commando do if he didn't have wire cutters to break through? Joseph takes a few steps back and runs at the high front gate, crashing into it with his shoulder like a fullback breaking loose into the end zone. Surprisingly, the rusted lock falls away, and the gate swings open. Weird, he thinks, how easily it gave way. Was the gate left half-open and not completely locked by a guard or owner who goes in and out regularly? Whatever, Joseph yells for the rabbi's sons to witness this small miracle, the open gate that his Bubby Sarah's daring and fearless spirit helped him achieve.

"That's great!" "Attaboy!" Shlomo and Danny are quick to gather up their bundles and join him at the open gate, but they stand there afraid to enter. "Go on in. What are you guys waiting for?" Joseph shouts.

"Wait! I don't think we should just walk in," Shlomo says, trying to convince his younger brother to hold back.

"Let him go first," Danny shouts. "We can say we just followed after Joseph. Unless he's too scared to go in by himself."

Joseph doesn't hesitate for a moment; he steps forward, leading them through the open gate. "You want to swim, don't you? So go swim!"

Joseph returns to the gate and carefully puts the rusted lock back in place. He decides to leave the gate ajar so it looks like it hadn't been broken into but as if it was hanging there at that funny angle, open to the public all the time despite the contrary big red signage. "We found the gate open, so we walked in to find a lifeguard or attendant to pay the entrance fee," he'd say if a police car drove by and an officer challenged them. Bubby Sarah would be proud of his American initiative. He laughs. And his Commando leaders would assure him it was exactly the right thing to do. You can't let artificial barriers stop you in time of war even if you have to step across peacetime boundaries and trespass. But looking back, he sees the rabbi's sons standing exactly where he left them, afraid to take a step closer toward the desired lakefront.

"Looks like the lake's been closed shut all summer long," Shlomo stammers. "Just look at the size of the weeds and those sunflowers. We could get into real trouble if Papa finds out we broke in. We should leave right now before anyone sees us."

"Hey, it's all right with me," Joseph says, doubly annoyed by the brothers sudden passivity. "Either way, whatever you want to do."

"Walk all the way back home in this heat for nothing?" Danny shouts. "No way! We're here to swim, aren't we?" Danny bolts forward a step or two, then hangs back waiting for Joseph to take the initiative.

An ominous feeling comes over Joseph as he leads the rabbi's sons slowly down the winding, twin-track, dirt driveway and past the men-and-women changing cabins toward the lakefront. Last year at Philips Lake, he recalls the loud sounds of splashing water and laughter from crowds of yelling little kids and teenagers fighting for a place in line to buy hot dogs, soda, ice cream, and candy bars. Today, the loud, fun noises are all missing; its changing rooms are boarded up and empty, everything inside the gated lake is overrun, deserted, and silent, and the realization that they are trespassing on illegal grounds begins to work on his fears. Any minute now the owner might appear with a shotgun and be furious with them, shoot a scare-away blast, or maybe call the police to have them arrested. Joseph begins to feel a bit fearful, having his own second thoughts. It feels increasingly eerie alone in the middle of the enormous, deserted lake property.

No one in sight, but the huge overgrown weeds and sunflowers take on almost human appearances as if they are tall sentries standing guard. Everywhere he looks, out along the distant edges of the glistening lake into the corner shallows, there are overgrown weeds…weeds everywhere they shouldn't be, weeds up to five feet tall, looking like real people. To Joseph, the surroundings take on the look of a bizarre military battleground, a dangerous lake and cow pastureland where overgrown weeds could be protecting an invisible enemy army, like the forest in Shakespeare's play that mysteriously comes alive to attack false Macbeth for killing the king. Around the water's edge, there may be snakes hidden beneath high grass—copperheads, black snakes, and maybe nests of poison spiders. Best to stay close along the winding dirt drive and bare sand pathways.

As the boys move closer, the lake water appears to have lost most of its beauteous diamond sparkle; it takes on a dark, murky look beneath the surface, and nowhere is its bottom visible. They stop a few feet from the ten-foot strip of sand around the lake shore, tentative still, making no enthusiastic attempt to cross the low concrete barrier and get any closer to the water. "Maybe it's not such a hot day after all," Shlomo says to Danny, adjusting his black yarmulke. "I don't think we should be in here. We should turn around and go back home to Papa's farmhouse." Even Joseph is starting to reconsider. The *Keep Out!* sign seems transposed, plastered across the face of the murky waters, regaining its original foreboding presence. *How strange a feeling,* Joseph thinks. *We're afraid to plunge forward, but even more embarrassed to turn back.*

Joseph feels as if an invisible evil spirit has lured them into what now seems a huge and scary, haunted garden—a place where the boys never really wanted to be in the first place. Why would a spirit have lured them in or made the lake look diamond-like and so attractive? Clearly, Philips Lake looked so much better from outside the fence than it does inside here along the deserted sand with the tall, silent, humanlike sunflowers.

Looming above the beach, a lifeguard's weather-stained high white chair stands empty, reminding Joseph of the dangers of swimming alone without an adult lifeguard to protect them. He reads the admonition aloud to the other boys: "No swimming allowed unless Lifeguard present." Joseph gazes out to the lone raft in the middle of the lake, then he looks south toward a spooky corner shallows, where as a four-year-old he'd been caught in its soft mud or quicksand and, unable to escape its downward draw, found himself sinking until he was almost chin deep in water.

He'd screamed out for his mother, but she couldn't hear him with the noise of other kids splashing and yelling. Miraculously, a crippled old man noticed and hobbled to the water's edge, his steps taking what seemed an eternity before offering the boy the end of his solid outstretched wooden cane and slowly pulled him up onto the solid beach. "No, it's wasn't really quicksand, just plain mud. The lifeguard showed me," his mother snapped. "So you would've been just fine if you stayed calm and paddled your way free of the mud. Lesson number one," she chided him, "You must learn never to panic." He'd worked hard at that lesson, learned to swim well enough to feel calm inside, nearly invincible around water; he'd been able to challenge the high ocean waves, currents and strong undertow for hours swimming in the Atlantic Ocean earlier this year.

"That water looks scary," Shlomo keeps saying. "Full of mud, and look at all those weeds." "Don't scare me," brags Danny. "You act like a little old lady, just like Papa says." Laughing in his older brother's face, Danny runs to the water's edge fully clothed, and he jumps back and forth from sand to water, kicking and splashing the lake water in Shlomo's direction.

"Stop it," Shlomo yells. "You'll ruin your pants and shoes. Mama will kill us both." Danny splashes him one more time before stopping to disrobe. The rabbi's sons undress in unison; they are both wearing old-fashioned dark brown bathing trunks under their pants. They carefully fold their black shirts and trousers and place them along with their walking shoes in two neat piles atop an old moldy-bottom rowboat that they discover overturned in high weeds behind the empty lifeguard's chair.

Meantime, Joseph tosses off his T-shirt and sneakers and shallow dives into the lake to avoid the weeds below the surface. He yells out at Danny, "I'll race you to the raft." Without looking back, Joseph sets out in his version of an Australian crawl, holding his breath for as many fast strokes as he can make rather than taking a systematic breath with every second or fourth stroke as the really good swimmers do. Pulling himself up onto the raft, Joseph looks back at the rabbi's sons; they are seated on the sandy beach, their backs turned toward him, beginning to build walled Austrian cities and castles off in a world of their own. Joseph lays his wet stomach down gently on the blistering-hot wooden raft and stretches out, closing his eyes and enjoying the feel of the relentless early afternoon sun as it bakes the dark-green lake water off his shoulders and back.

Lying in the middle of the vast deserted lake, the boy has a sense of being in the center of the universe—his image being the Garden of Eden transformed across time. Concerns about trespassing and guilt have all disappeared. In fact, Joseph feels a special pleasure once more at having stepped through an invisible glass wall of law and restrictions and broken through to a place where ordinary people are not allowed to go. On shore, the rabbi's sons look content playing in the sand; he listens to their muted laughter. Going for a swim has turned out to be a pretty good idea after all, though it's a one-time lucky event that he won't try to repeat.

A moment later, Joseph begins to have doubts once more, wary that the owner or police might hear or see them and come roaring through the gate to arrest them. Can they be fined? he wonders. His father will kill him if they were. These are very tough times economically; his father's patients are paying off their bills a little bit at a time, and with the new babies, his mother says, they're having problems getting by. He'd better swim back to shore now to tell the rabbi's sons to keep their voices and laughter down because sounds seem to resonate in this deserted watery playground like in an echo chamber. Yet he decides to wait a few minutes before swimming in to confront them. All is so still and peaceful at the lake that for one of the first times all summer, Joseph truly forgets about war and his fear of Nazis, even the need to keep up his Commando training.

He lowers himself gently into the water and floats on his back then begins to paddle slowly, using his body as a small craft. He is enjoying the warmth of the sun's strong rays on his face and stomach as he paddles out across midlake for several minutes before turning back toward the beach. Beneath his naked back, hidden underwater, Joseph feels clusters of weeds rising up from the muddy bottom and licking at his body as he paddles by. He recalls hearing that Philips is a man-made lake developed by the farmer from his lower thirty acres of cow pastures and grazing fields—a body of water that needs to be drained and bulldozed early each spring to keep its bottom clear of fast-growing underbrush. Still, the boy is surprised by the number and size of weeds his body encounters as he paddles on his back toward shore. He notices that the rabbi's sons don't really join in swimming but run in and out of the lake every so often, splash about, then dart back to their sand castles along the beach laughing. All they really need is a hose and kiddies' pool to jump in and out of. *I've got to tell them not to be so loud. And insist that we leave soon.* But they seem so content that he decides to let them alone to play a little while longer in this surprisingly peaceful Garden of Eden.

Rising from the lake, Joseph stretches his body several times before climbing up onto the high lifeguard's chair to scout the distant fields and roads for any sign of the owner or of a passing police car. A large crow or blackbird catches his eye, soaring twice across the lake and off beyond the pastureland to the southeast. Following the crow, his eyes come to rest, focused on the motion of a young boy crossing the distant southerly road. The boy pauses along the wire fence and seems to be gazing right across the lake in their direction. A momentary chill passes over Joseph. Could the boy be the owner's son or one of their family? If so, will he call his father to chase them? Odd the way the boy stands motionless at the fence for so long a time, the angle of his head and eyes definitely focused in the direction of Joseph and the rabbi's sons. To move out of his direct sightline, Joseph jumps off the lifeguard's chair onto the beach, feeling a jolt of pain from his swollen ankle. Time to leave; it's not a good idea to be caught inside this lake, where they really don't belong.

"Someone's coming. We'd better get out of here," Joseph yells as he limps across the sand toward Shlomo and Danny, who are hard at work improving their elegant group of sand castles and moats.

"Give us artists a few minutes more, and we'll finish up," Shlomo replies. "Who's coming?" asks Danny. "I don't see anyone."

Joseph climbs back up onto the high lifeguard chair and looks south across the lake; the motionless boy is no longer at the fence. He's gone out of sight. Maybe he wasn't staring at them, or maybe he just stopped to look then went on his way. So Joseph scrambles down to the beach to join the rabbi's sons and begins to sculpt a complex of army fortifications, reservoirs and canals. Lying on his stomach, legs dangling into the water's edge, Joseph loses all sense of time while creating his own neat world of war-related architectural miniatures out of the wet sand.

Minutes later, a dark shadow cuts across the edge of his canals. Joseph looks up surprised to see the boy from the distant fence just a few feet away from him in the surf, removing his T-shirt and sneakers, and dousing his body with lake water. No question, the boy must have been watching them and found his way in through the rusty gate that Joseph had deliberately left part open. The thin blondish-haired boy squats down in the shallows and continues to splash muddy lake water all over his body, head, and hair while emitting heavy-breathing, asthmatic sounds as he splashes. Strange, Joseph thinks, how he almost magically appeared alongside them, but he's made no attempt to interact or even introduce himself. His sudden, unannounced presence is disturbing to Joseph. Both Shlomo and Danny also seem wary, watching the new boy out of the corners of their eyes without confronting him directly.

"Hi there! Hello," Joseph yells out in a friendly way simply to break the ice and acknowledge his presence. The boy takes his time answering, first shaking lake water off his body like a dog might do before sloshing his way across the shallows toward Joseph.

"You're not supposed to be swimming here, you know," the boy states in a slow, neutral rather than confrontational voice. "Lake's closed. Didn't you see the No Trespassing sign on the gate?"

The boy's assertive tone sets Joseph on guard. "Well, I guess you must be trespassing too?"

The boy thinks about it for a moment. "I think maybe I'm allowed. My father knows the owner."

"The owner lets you swim here without a lifeguard?"

Oddly, the boy doesn't bother to answer; he simply turns away, jogs over to the tall lifeguard's chair, and begins a series of pull-ups, counting quietly to himself. His actions and intent are hard for Joseph to read as he closely watches the boy's bicep muscles rise, tighten, and flex during his exercises. The boy seems about Joseph's age; while thin, he has a square face, a strong jaw, and his muddy-blond hair is crew cut. He doesn't seem to be showing off for them with his series of pull-ups; it's more like a ritual or training regimen that the boy practices without really thinking about who, if anyone, may be watching. Joseph is impressed by the boy's muscles and stamina, but his odd, aggressive behavior is worrisome. His unpredictable actions convey to Joseph an unspoken physical challenge.

The boy glances over at the rabbi's sons, who've turned their backs and are muttering in Yiddish, arguing about how to complete their elegant sand creations. After his series of exercises, the boy hops down from the tall lifeguard's chair and wanders over to the rabbi's sons to see what they're doing. He stands above them, staring down at their castles far too long, making them uncomfortable at his lack of comment. Shlomo finally looks up at him nervously while Danny edges away, a bit frightened by the boy's all-too-silent closeness.

Suddenly, they all hear a loud burst of noise and sounds of raucous laughter as three older boys appear, trotting down the driveway toward the lakefront together, exchanging lots of small talk and banter, but acting as if they belong here. The three are wearing bathing briefs and appear to have come by way of the stone house out by the road, formerly a bar and grill, that is fenced off, separate from the lake but leased out by the farmer. All three older boys ignore Joseph and the others completely; they splash dive into the lake and race each other in a fast swim out to the raft. They are athletic, very good swimmers, and they arrive at the raft in a near dead heat. After pulling themselves up onto the wooden raft and resting there a while, they begin playing a roughhouse, king-of-the-mountain game, wrestling and pushing each other off the raft while laughing, cursing, and yelling in a friendly but competitive game. A little later, after taking a few minutes rest to sun themselves, the boys decide to dive off the raft and race back to shore.

The tallest, a dark-haired boy, dries himself off with a small hand towel, and stares at Shlomo and Danny in their black yarmulkes; when the rabbi's sons notice, he grins self-consciously and nods at them, acting as if he is admiring their elegant European castles. Then, without comment, he rejoins his two rough comrades, and all three march up the dirt driveway exchanging constant shoulder bumps and friendly chatter. They are gone back toward the stone house without having said a word about the younger boys' illegal presence. Very strange, thinks Joseph, but their lack of a challenge makes him feel a bit more comfortable. *The older boys saw us sculpting castles and moats in the sand and probably figured since we aren't swimming, we aren't hurting anyone by being here on the beach even if the lake is closed and we are all illegals. Maybe one of them is part of the owner's family, probably not, or he surely would have lectured us about no swimming allowed without a proper lifeguard on hand.*

"Hey! You're stepping all over my canals. Stop it!" Joseph yells up at the blond boy. Maybe he hadn't noticed, but the boy stumbled over parts of Joseph's miniature waterworks right next to his buildings. He steps away, but doesn't say he's sorry or say anything at all. The thin blondish boy just stands there silently as if trying to understand what Joseph is constructing and where his sandy domain starts and ends. Well, maybe his action wasn't intentional. Maybe the boy's just a little slow to figure things out.

"Okay," the boy finally says, "but you don't own all of that sand."

Once again, the way he says it is more neutral than confrontational. The blond boy returns to the high lifeguard's chair, climbing up and hanging by his legs, off doing still another round of his bodybuilding exercises. He acts as if he is bored and just tumbling about, trying to find something to do. Joseph remains wary but decides it's safe to ignore the boy; he returns to patching up his damaged canals and improving his army fortress and its outlying buildings. A short time later, Joseph is startled to hear a very loud scraping, banging sound from behind the lifeguard's chair; then Shlomo's shouting begins in earnest.

"You idiot! What are you doing!" Shlomo screams out.

The blond boy found the moldy rowboat behind the lifeguard's chair and managed to turn it right-side-up, in the process knocking the brothers' carefully folded shirts and pants into the weeds as if he hadn't even noticed them. Shlomo and Danny run over to confront him, "That's our good clothes you knocked on the ground!" "Oh yeah," he says, acting surprised. Then he mumbles, "So what?" "What do you mean 'so what'?"

The boy thinks for a moment then says, "I'm playing with this here rowboat. Maybe I'm gonna take the rowboat out into the lake. Any of you guys got a problem with that?"

Shlomo decides to back off, picking up their clothes and refolding them. "If you called us first, we'd of come over and moved our clothes."

"Yeah," says Danny, "you don't just knock other people's clothes all over the ground. Okay?"

The thin blondish boy stands alongside the boat, glaring out at the rabbi's sons without saying a word. Then he gets into the rowboat and gathers up the oars. He acts as if the rowboat is his personal possession, and maybe they had no right putting their clothes on it in the first place. Shlomo and Danny decide to retreat; they take their clothes closer to their sculpture area, placing two neat piles on the cement divider between the twin pathways and the sand.

Joseph feels he has to get involved; he can't let this pushy local boy walk all over his grandfather's Jewish renters even if the blond boy is good at exercising and has more muscles than he has. He approaches the boy, who is sitting inside the moldy old rowboat, wiping off one of its muddy oars with a handful of large green leaves. Joseph doesn't want to start trouble, but he can't just walk away from the boy's provocative action.

"You think that rowboat's yours?" Joseph asks.

"Maybe it is," the boy answers, not looking up.

"What does 'maybe' mean? You think it's yours or not?"

The boy stares up at Joseph, once more for several beats too long. "I guess you're with them, right? You're one of those guys, aren't you?" he asks in a peculiar, demeaning way.

"Sure, we all came here together if that's what you mean."

"They're religious, aren't they, wearing those black skullcaps? Are they—?" he stops in midsentence.

"Yep, their father's a rabbi. A Jewish rabbi? You're right," Joseph says, confirming his view that the boy is a little bit slow for his age.

"You don't wear a skullcap? Are they your cousins from the City?"

"Nope, we're not related at all," Joseph says. "They been renting my grandfather's farmhouse this summer. It's a few miles away on Hempstead. We've got a farm with lots of chickens. We used to have a cow and a goat. My folks and I have lived on the farm most of my life, and I go to school in town here. You get it now?"

He said too much and wonders why he had to explain it all to the boy. Sure, he brought the rabbi's sons here, but he needs to separate himself from the soft City renters, who wear yarmulkes even on the beach. Well, he isn't exactly a farm boy himself; he feels part of a number of different worlds, although he does have Jewish cousins who come up once or twice a year from Long Island. And Grandfather's family did live downtown in the Village on Bleecker Street when they first came over from the old country, and Grandfather was a health inspector in New York City before becoming a farmer and building lots of chicken coops, a home and apartment from the large barn out back, and then their own family's bungalow. Joseph's father isn't a farmer. He is different—a professional man, a scholarship winner, very unlike most of their neighbors. It is not easy for Joseph to figure exactly which culture he belongs to, but he doesn't want this blond boy to pigeonhole him as "one of them." In a basic way, that question challenges his manhood and his quest to be a different kind of Jew, a modern American Jew like his mother, able to train himself to become a real Commando with the will and courage to someday face a platoon of Hitler youth. "The kind of man you can trust alongside you in a foxhole," as his Uncle Jacob speaks of all the ROTC buddies and officers he admires.

"What about you? You live around here?" Joseph asks. "Where do you come from?

"The Valley. My dad's the youngest sergeant on the Valley Police Force. What's yours do?"

"My father's an eye doctor. He's too old for the Army, they say, with two little babies at home. Is your dad too old for the Draft?"

"He wants to enlist in the Marines, but they won't let him. My uncle, Dad's young brother's a Marine in the Pacific. He's out there fighting the Japs on Guadalcanal or one of those islands where Japs troops are dug into bunkers. You know, I'll bet you he's out there right this minute while we're talkin' here facing real Jap machine gun bullets an' artillery shell explosions! Can you believe it?"

"That's great! My aunt's an Army nurse in Sicily. She was in Tunisia, North Africa, fighting Nazis and General Rommel in all those tank battles," Joseph says tentatively, wanting to take it back the moment he says it.

"Nurses don't fight anyone," the boy says, laughing at Joseph. "They don't let girls anywhere near a battlefield, my uncle says. An' he knows. He's one tough ole Leatherneck. He can shoot a rifle even better than my dad." The boy talks in a neutral, matter-of-fact tone without a competitive edge, but it seems clear that he is not impressed with Joseph's family of nurses and eye doctors. He finally thinks to introduce himself, "Hey, I'm Raymond." And Joseph follows suit. The boys decide they're almost the same age, ten an a half years old, and while a bit fuzzy, Raymond may be a class behind Joseph in elementary school.

"Hey, help me get this rowboat into the water," Raymond says enthusiastically. "I want to see if this old boat can float."

Raymond explains how he loves boats. His father and uncle used to rent their own powerboats on weekends and go deep-sea fishing in Long Island Sound miles out into the Atlantic Ocean and take him with them. When they returned home, they'd throw all the fish into a big laundry tub in their basement and give most of the big fish away to their friends and neighbors.

Joseph is envious of Raymond having a policeman as a father and a tough Marine uncle fighting the Japs in the Pacific. Sure, he's training himself to be a Commando someday, but his watchtower on the roof, his cornfield battleground, and underground cave in the forest are only make believe. Raymond's people are the real warriors, the kind of true American heroes the rest of us are counting on to win the war against the vicious, heavily armed Nazi and Jap soldiers. His uncle's out there in a foxhole on an island all muddy, and maybe bleeding, facing artillery and machine gun blasts with real bullets flying, fighting for us all. Not training or playing war games like Joseph does or renting country farmhouses like the rabbi and his sons, praying a lot and pretending to be nature lovers. Didn't Raymond ask "Are you one of them?" No, he's definitely not! He's in the process of becoming the real thing too, if he can find the courage and willpower within himself. He's got to find it; he can't let the Hitler youth bully and chase him off the streets like they did to his friend Peter and are doing to the Jews in Germany, Poland, and all across Europe.

But Joseph hesitates a moment, recalling the day he was ambushed in the sandpile and stoned, when his whole class had to stay after school because of him being late and he wound up having to fight all the tough kids in his class one after another. Well, he wasn't even eight years old then, and he was caught by surprise. All that happened before the war, two and a half years ago, before he began serious physical training. Joseph's mother, he knows, is tough and has a strong will, as does her mother, Bubby Sarah, and her ROTC brother, Jacob. But Joseph's father and grandfather have a kind of softness about them, and maybe he has a lot of that too. Well, everyone's scared going into battle, the older boys say; you've got to rely on your training, follow orders, and just move ahead and do it. He imagines himself going into battle alongside Raymond, this son of a policeman and nephew of a fighting Marine, to prove he has the same toughness to face Nazi and Jap bullets as any of them. While still riddled with self-doubt, he focuses on David, the Jewish boy in the Bible, who was fearless in the face of the giant, Goliath, and he prays to God to give him that kind of courage—the courage to back off from no one!

Meanwhile, the two boys are having a difficult time pushing the heavy old rowboat out of the weeds and across a wet crevice in the sand and into Philips Lake. Joseph looks at Raymond closely; they are pretty much the same size. Maybe he can grow up to be just as muscular and tough as this Marine's nephew seems to be if he works hard and is able to possess that mysterious thing called "character." *And maybe he has some advantages over the blond boy after all, his "smarts"—his creative ideas, quick strategic instincts, and his ability to concentrate.* He knows that he'll have to prove himself to true patriots like Raymond, his father, and his uncle. Now is a good time to start.

The rowboat is still stuck in a rut in the sand, so Joseph yells over for Danny to help, and the younger brother reluctantly joins them. As if taking up an unspoken challenge, Raymond starts to boss the two boys around, pointing Joseph to the bow and Danny to the far side. "Now let's push! Push harder!" Raymond gives orders in a naturally commanding voice. Pushing and straining awkwardly, the three boys are finally able to slide the boat out of its sandy knot and into the water.

"Watch out now. Stand clear," Raymond orders, ankle deep in the shallows, pulling the boat free by its bow and into the lake. The boys watch as the old rowboat takes on the life it was designed for, bobbing back and forth on the lake surface and reflecting glints of majestic afternoon sunlight. All thoughts of whether it's sound and can stay afloat disappear. "Hey! Help me in," Raymond orders. The two boys help him climb aboard while holding the bobbing rowboat still. Raymond takes up an oar and stands upright, smiling broadly as he makes the rowboat rock back and forth in the surf.

Seeing Raymond balance himself in the bobbing rowboat, Joseph is troubled at being bossed about and by the arrogant way that Raymond is acting—as if he owns the old rowboat as well as being its captain. *Maybe he won't even invite us aboard, just ask us to push him up and down the shorefront. Sure, it was Raymond's idea to salvage the boat, turn it upright, and take it out into the lake, but we all chipped in to make that happen. Without us, it would still be stuck in the weeds.* And now he's taken on an arrogant, possessive attitude that is disturbing to Joseph.

"Hey! Hand me the other oar," Raymond orders Danny, still in a neutral way. "Right there in the weeds. Are you blind or something?"

"Where are you planning to take this old boat?" Joseph asks.

"I dunno. Anywhere I feel like, I guess." He giggles in a self-conscious but not at all arrogant way. You could almost like Raymond when he giggles that way, Joseph thinks. Well, Raymond has taken full possession of the rowboat, but he seems uncertain about what to do next.

A battleground idea comes to Joseph which he instantly volunteers before really thinking it through. "You like war games, I'll bet," Joseph says. "Let's play a war game, okay? This rowboat's a PT boat or maybe a small US destroyer." His idea is out there and takes on a life of its own before he can change anything. Joseph senses that he is challenging himself to take command in hopes that Raymond, and maybe Danny as well, will follow his lead. "We'll take the boat out like you said. Only let's make believe this beach is North Africa, and mainland Italy's way over there across the lake. Nazi and Italian gunners are hiding there waiting to wipe out the Americans. No, way across there," he points. "We can't see them, but their guns and soldiers are hiding in that bunch of trees in the middle of the cow pasture. Let's see if we can take this bombed-out, crippled old PT boat that the Nazis thought they'd destroyed and never expected to see afloat again, and take her clear across the lake. We'll sneak over and attack their outpost by surprise and clear the coast for the American invasion."

Raymond and Danny look across the lake to the distant pastureland, which seems much too far, an ocean away. It even seems a long way to Joseph now that he studies the distance. "Well, what do you guys think?" Joseph asks. "Too hard a mission?" Raymond seems to have brightened at the idea of playing a war game, but he isn't responding one way or the other. *Maybe because it's my idea,* Joseph thinks, *and not his own.*

Shlomo overhears Joseph and splashes over in the shallows, yelling to his brother. "Don't do it!" Shlomo cries out. "Crossing over's a crazy idea, a dangerous idea. Anyway, you and I got to leave now," he yells at younger brother, Danny. "Come on, let them play whatever crazy war game they want to play. We can find our own way home."

"He's right. You don't have to go with us," Joseph reassures Danny. "It is a dangerous mission. And you don't like war games anyway." Danny stares across the lake with trepidation, but he doesn't want to give in to Shlomo, whose own father says acts like a little old lady.

"Suppose the rowboat can't make it across and sinks," Shlomo argues. "You can't swim well enough to make it all the way back."

"Wait up," Joseph agrees. "If you're not a good swimmer, no way we can let you on our handpicked Commando team."

"Shaddup! I can swim as good as anyone!" Danny says, biting his lower jaw.

"Okay, show us," Joseph responds, nodding at Raymond who is simply an observer now, not trying to lead anymore.

Danny takes the challenge and sets off dog-paddling along the shore, "Look! I can keep this up for hours, across the lake and back."

Maybe he can, and maybe he can't, but at least it looks like he can safely stay afloat. Joseph turns to Raymond. "What do you think? Is Danny a good enough swimmer to be part of our Commando mission?" "Sure, why not." Raymond giggles. "In real Commando raids," Joseph adds, "they say your team is only as good as your weakest link." Nevertheless, it seems settled. Danny will be part of their team if he wants it that badly. Shlomo begins to curse in Yiddish, but his younger brother ignores him. Danny is now part of this bigger, all-American goyisha war game, an approved member of the PT boat's crew.

Pulling himself up and over the side, Joseph climbs into the stern of the bobbing rowboat. Danny reaches out for help, and Joseph pulls the lighter boy aboard. "Whoa, boat's taking in water. Too much weight with both of you on board," Raymond mutters from the bow, acting like he's still the Captain in charge.

Joseph hopes to stay in charge. He sees a rusty old coffee can in the weeds on the shore near where the rowboat once rested. "Wait a minute." He leaps off the boat to retrieve the coffee can then returns and begins to bail the water off the floorboards. "I'll bet that's why the coffee can was sitting there alongside the boat." The leak is very slow, so he easily bails the water out faster than it's coming in.

Shlomo wades out alongside the rowboat, making a pest of himself. "Look! It's leaking already. No way this moldy old rowboat can make it across the lake. Come on, Danny, don't force me to pull you out."

Joseph is getting irritated now. The war game was his idea, a way to get aboard the rowboat and share the fun, put himself in charge, maybe, and lead Raymond. The real war game is between himself and Raymond, a test to see whether he can match up with this physical boy whose father is a cop and whose uncle is a Marine fighting Japs in the Pacific, all tough, macho men who took Raymond out on their deep-sea fishing trips since he was a young kid. Can he hold his own and win respect from these kind of people, Joseph wonders, let alone become a leader? Danny is soft, and his very presence is getting in the way, a city boy who wears a yarmulke and dog-paddles like a girl.

"Why don't you get off the boat before we start?" Joseph orders. "Go home with your brother. I think Raymond and I can handle the mission without you." He looks over at Raymond, who nods. "Sure, the boat'll ride better if he gets off!"

But Danny is too stubborn and digs in. He won't listen to anyone. "Leave me alone. I'm part of the game too!" he yells out. Shlomo finally gives up, curses him in Yiddish, and wades back to shore.

"Okay, you guys, it's time to push off," Joseph commands, grabbing one of the oars from Raymond in the bow and pushing off from the stern like the oarsmen in Venice he's seen in the cinema. "You handle bailing," he orders Danny, handing him the coffee can. "Why can't I row?" Danny protests, but Joseph ignores him.

The mission is underway just as Joseph envisioned it. But as the rowboat turns and moves out from shore, the distant pastureland looks far away, a great blue expanse of lake between them. *It might be too far for us to travel safely on a rowboat already taking in water. Well, no problem. We can always turn back,* Joseph thinks *or dive off and swim back. If the PT boat starts to sink, we'll just let the old boat go under.* He laughs to himself, wondering what the owner will think finding his missing rowboat sunk way out on the bottom of the lake.

"Do you think we can make it all the way across?" Danny yells out, staring at the distant pastureland, his coffee can idle.

"We can do it, if you keep bailing harder!" Joseph hollers back. Yet when Danny returns to bailing, he notices that the stream of leaking water seems to be increasing slightly faster than the younger boy can bail.

Meanwhile, Raymond keeps paddling methodically in the bow, intent on the goal, hardly looking back or saying a word. It pleases Joseph that his war game has begun and that he has quietly taken command; the other two boys seem content to follow his orders and try to achieve the difficult mission he defined. They must be feeling the same excitement he's feeling. Rising to the dramatic moment, Joseph springs to his feet in the stern with an oar in hand and finds himself yelling out "Yaaah!" in boyish exuberance, imagining to himself that they are part of General George Washington's band of brave American conscripts crossing the Delaware and surprising the British by boldly attacking the Hessian forces at Trenton. Danny stares up at him as if he is going crazy, but that doesn't bother Joseph; his job is to keep their focus on the destination. He begins imagining how the Nazi forces across the lake have positioned their guns and soldiers to protect the Italian shoreline from the American invasion forces.

"Our plan," he hollers, "is to disembark, separate, and hit the ground. Then we start crawling, sneaking up on the enemy who are hiding in that cluster of trees. When I give the signal, I'll whistle. We'll jump up and surprise attack together and wipe out the Nazi and Italian machine guns guarding against the American landing before they know what hit them." It's too bad, he thinks, that they don't have BB guns to make it more realistic; he'll tell them to break off sticks for rifles as soon as they hit shore.

Suddenly, Joseph remembers the distant shore as muddy; they might have to jump out early and wade in. He hopes there is no quicksand on that shoreline to deal with, but he decides not to mention possible quicksand to the others. After defeating the enemy, they can leave the old rowboat on the far shore and circle back around the lake by foot before celebrating their victory and starting home. No reason to risk rowing the leaking boat all the way back across the lake to the lifeguard's chair. Let the owner find his old boat on the far shore and wonder how it could have drifted clear across the lake by itself. He'd like to be there to see the old farmer's face. But now, he hears Raymond grunting loudly, and Joseph becomes aware that rowing the boat forward is getting a heck of a lot tougher.

In fact, their Commando mission is getting almost nowhere. Fifteen minutes or more have passed and the boat is less than a third of the way across the lake to the pasture landing in their game to catch the dangerous Nazi and Italian soldiers by surprise. But it is difficult to paddle faster since both their oars keep catching in clusters of weeds just below the surface, slowing them down and jerking them off course in irregular directions whenever an oar catches. His own arms are getting tired, and Danny keeps complaining that bailing is too hard and often stops to rest.

"Hey! We've got to paddle faster but make shallower strokes in the water. And let's try to row together more in unison!" he yells ahead to Raymond, who barely turns to acknowledge his order. Maybe he should call a time out to give everyone a few minutes of needed rest. Just then, Joseph feels a subtle surge in the flow of water beneath his feet. The surge is followed by a second flow of water that spurts out from a new slit in the tar between two floorboards and quickly spreads, beginning to fill the bottom of the old rowboat with lake water in only a few seconds.

"Quick, give me the bailing can!" he yells to Danny, grabbing it out of the younger boy's hands, and he notices the frightened look on his face.

"We sprung a big leak!" Danny screams out. "I'm getting off!"

Joseph bails furiously with the coffee can, trying to catch up and get ahead of the dangerous new flow, but water keeps streaming in more quickly than he can deal with as the cracks on the tar bottom widen. All at once, the boat lurches sharply to one side as Danny jumps overboard and clings to the inland side of the boat. "Let go! You're pulling us all down. Swim to shore," Joseph orders. He feels the boat release and rebalance and assumes Danny is on his way, dog-paddling back to safety.

"Help me bail! Our PT boat's in real trouble. We're starting to sink!" he yells out to Raymond who turns to Joseph, not seeming to know what to do, a frustrated look crossing his face. "I need you to help me bail!" Joseph repeats, screaming the words out. Raymond nods his head, drops his oar against the oarlock, and begins bailing the water awkwardly with his two cupped hands.

"We gotta bail even faster!" Joseph yells. Yet as furiously as the two boys are bailing, the inflow of lake water through the new cracks in the seams is too much for them. The water level is rising high up onto his ankles. It is instantly clear to Joseph that there is no way they can keep the sinking rowboat afloat much longer. If the water level rises much further, the boat will suddenly plunge underwater!

Sensing a critical moment of command, Joseph excitedly cries out, "Abandon ship! Abandon ship!" He rises to full height, steps up onto the shaky center crossbeam, steadies his body, and takes in a deep breath then dives off the stern toward shore, knowing that he's ordered the right action at just the right moment—the only sensible command possible. As his body hits the water, Joseph hears a crashing noise from the bow behind him that sounds like an oar hitting an oarlock or the side of the rowboat. Joseph's dive is clean but much too deep. Stupid! He should have dived flatter, more of a racing dive; in his hyperexcitement, he has propelled his body far too deep into the dangerous waters, and he feels his belly scraping along the muddy lake bottom thick with weeds.

Joseph has dived so deep under the dark muddy water that he is unable to see his own hands as his body glides into one cluster of dark underwater weeds after another. Increasingly, he feels himself becoming enwrapped in long stems whose leaves reach out and curl themselves around his arms and shoulders. The harder he fights to free himself, the more the weeds entwine and lock him in their arms. He'd taken a deep breath before diving, but he feels it starting to run out. Should he let his breath out even for a second or two, the lake water will rush into his lungs and smother him. Drowning can happen within a few seconds of exhaling, he's heard. Locked in, trapped by the weeds, he begins to panic.

He sees the image of his mother's angry face alongside him in the waters, his mind focusing on his quicksand accident years before in the shallows of this same lake. What was it his mother told him? "Be calm, don't panic. Find a way to work yourself free!" Well, there's no choice now. Either work yourself free or drown.

Instinctively, he curls his body into a ball, its most compact form, and lets himself drop down toward lake bottom. Then, one by one, trying not to rush, Joseph begins to pull off each clinging, knotted weed until his arms and shoulders have worked free of their grasp. Next, he forces his bent knees and legs down to the muddy bottom of the lake, his hands pushing up against the water's pressure, and he springs upward with as powerful a leg thrust as he's able to generate. And fantastic! His face lifts out of the muddy lake barely in time for him to take in a huge gulp of air before he goes under for a second time. Pushing aside more weeds, he floats up to the surface, emerging only about ten feet from where he originally dove in. Treading water, breathing hard, he catches sight of the rowboat submerged in the lake with its bow at a weird upward angle and its oars floating free. Just as he reaches out for one of the oars, a loud crescendo of boyish screams echo across the water's surface.

Disoriented at first, he can't tell which direction to look. Then he spots a frantic Shlomo standing chest deep off shore, waving and screaming at him to help his brother. But where? Joseph doesn't see Danny at first. Yet Shlomo keeps pointing hysterically; only then does he glimpse the back of a head floating between them. Joseph begins to glide toward the head using breaststrokes to keep his own body high in the water well above the clutching weeds. After a few quick strokes, he reaches Danny, who is floundering in water too deep to stand. He drops underwater behind the younger boy's backside and pushes him in toward shore then under again, repeating the process until they're close enough to stand, and he lifts the boy's half-submerged head. Danny is thrashing about and coughing out water, so Joseph squeezes his belly from behind, then whacks him on his shoulders and back, while all the time walking him in, edging his body into the shallows where his big brother, Shlomo, is waiting to wrap him into a large beach towel.

Danny and his towel are dropped face down in the sand, crushing what was one of their finest sand castles. His brother jumps astride his back, rhythmically trying to press the lake water out of his system until young Danny, who is coughing repeatedly, is finally able to scream out,

"Stop! Enough! Get off my back. I can't breathe!" All this time, Shlomo has been cursing Danny in Yiddish, praying to God and thanking Yahweh that Danny has survived and even blessing Joseph once in English for coming to the rescue and helping him save his reckless young brother's life.

Totally exhausted, Joseph sprawls out on the sand trying to unwind and relax his shaking muscles from the ordeal of the rowboat's sinking and his underwater escape from the dangerous, clinging weeds. He thinks about the futility of their failed war mission. *Stupid! All so dumb!* He lets his mind go blank, closes his irritated eyes, and begins to inhale the fine, hot midsummer air into his lungs in a series of deep Yoga breaths.

The sun's heat radiates across the lake, its light creating a series of white ripples. Joseph's eyes blink at the throbbing light, trying to focus; the images in his mind's eye blur and mix together. He attempts to see more clearly, to comprehend the exciting but scary, warlike action that just took place. He relives a vision of the rowboat sinking, but the picture of its bow pointing upward out of the lake continues to throb in the light and strain his eyesight. An impenetrable motion or thought passes before his eyes, and Joseph has a sense of being half-blind, constantly missing its meaning. Calmer now after Danny's near drowning and Shlomo's loud, emotional outbursts, the three boys huddle close to each other on the sandy beach and stare out at the implacable lake.

In that still moment, Joseph's world revolves to a silent resting place. Time itself has stopped, nothing moves, and there's no sound or sign of life. He tries to focus clearly on the lake despite the constant throbbing motion of sunlight upon the waters. Joseph forces his swollen eyes to move slowly and methodically across the watery surface, carefully approaching the bow of the rowboat sticking out high above the smooth, rippling water with its two wooden oars floating close-by, their broad edges, in some odd way, connected to the source of the light's bouncing reflections. Joseph's mind is troubled and fragmented, its scattered pieces refusing to meld together; instead of clarity, there is a logjam, like trying to understand a complex mathematics problem for the first time and being unable to break through the fog with the simplest perspective.

All at once, loud shouting shatters the silence of the lakefront. It is the voices of the three older roughhouse boys calling out to them as they return in a fast trot down the dirt driveway. They heard Shlomo's original screams and have come running back down to the lake to find out what's wrong. Confronted, Shlomo explains to them that the younger boys tried to take the rowboat across the lake.

"Idiots!" the skinny one breaks in. "That old mother's so full of cracks I wouldn't trust her to float across a puddle. Our lifeguard was told to scrap her two years ago." His tall, dark-haired friend breaks in with a concerned voice. "But everyone's all right; all of you are safe and well now?"

Joseph is eager to assure him they are all okay, but the words fail to come out of his mouth. Instead, a rumbling sound begins in his stomach. He looks out over the stillness of the lake one more time, yet this time he trembles, frightened to see nothing but streaks of light across the gently lapping waters. Absence has suddenly become a cause for horror. Joseph holds his breath and looks again as if for the first time, and he begins to painfully realize what is missing. He feels an oversized tumor working its way up from deep inside his stomach; he begins to tremble as it makes its toxic journey up his entire being, leaving in its wake an incredibly stunned look on his face.

"What is it? Tell me!" the tall boy demands, grabbing Joseph and shaking him by his shoulders.

But Joseph is shivering now, tongue-tied; all this can't be happening in real life! *Yes, God help us, a third boy was with us aboard the rowboat. How can it possibly be that I never noticed till this moment that Raymond is missing?* At that precise moment, Shlomo, remembers too and screams out to the tall boy in his high-pitched, emotional voice, "There was another boy... another boy on the rowboat!" Shlomo gestures to the older boys, his voice choking "And he's not here!"

All heads and eyes swing back to the gently lapping lake water, which looks benign and undisturbed, its harmony broken only by the angular bow of a rowboat pointing upward and two idle oars floating nearby. The sight of an undisturbed lake surface makes all the boys pale and sicken. Joseph lurches toward the lifeguard's chair and begins to throw up in dry heaves. A moment later, gaining control, Joseph's eyes suddenly light up, and he finds himself shouting, "I'll bet he's hiding. Raymond's playing a joke on all of us. He must be hiding somewhere!"

Joseph moves quickly into action on his hunch. *I got to be right! Raymond swam over to the close-by raft for safety, and he's been hiding behind the raft all this time probably laughing at us all for not noticing his absence.* Joseph sets off running around the circular lakefront to get to a point where he'll be able to see behind the raft. Meantime, two of the older boys throw off their shirts, wade into the lake and swim in strong, athletic strokes toward the sunken rowboat while the tall, dark-haired boy races back up the driveway to summon help. After running halfway around the lake, Joseph is finally able to look behind the lone raft, but he sees no one hiding there, only dark lake water lapping, forever lapping at its base. He waits an extra beat in time in case Raymond is still trying to fool him by diving underneath the wooden raft and holding his breath when he saw Joseph coming. "No one's behind the raft!" Joseph yells loudly enough for the two rescue boys to hear him across the lake. His mind keeps spinning out one denial after another. "What about the changing rooms?"

That's it! Raymond must have swam to shore while he and Shlomo were helping to save Danny, and he's hiding in the men's room or, even better, hiding in the women's room to fool them completely. But when Joseph arrives at the changing rooms out of breath, he finds both doors bolted shut as he should have remembered they were, and there is no one hiding behind the shacks in the grove of fir trees. *No, none of this makes any sense! Raymond wouldn't just run off by himself and go home. He'd want to meet up with us, with his war game team, so we could all talk excitedly together about the rowboat's sinking and talk about Danny dog-paddling so feebly that he couldn't make it to shore on his own.* Sure, they'd have a good chuckle together over Danny's brave talk.

Fighting off total denial, Joseph's legs turn weak and shaky, and a dizziness comes over him—a sense that the whole world's gone mad with images of bodies lurching back and forth across a lakefront totally out of balance. "Nothing can be as it seems!" His frantic mind keeps racing ahead toward an impossible reality, and there's no way he can stop it! If Raymond has vanished, disappeared, and he isn't hiding behind the raft or in one of the changing rooms, where could he possibly be? "No, please God, not down there underneath the lapping waters, his arms and legs caught up in the weeds!" The enormity of that horrifying final image was too much for the boy's mind to contemplate.

Stumbling back to the lakefront near the high, empty lifeguard's chair, his own body out of balance, Joseph encounters a picture he prayed he'd never see, one that he'd never escape from as long as he lives. The two older boys, who were diving feverishly in the waters around the rowboat, come together all at once and emerge from the lake carrying a limp small, purplish-blue form between them. "We had to pull his body out of weeds!" they scream in unison. Rushing ashore, they place the limp form gently facedown on what was once Shlomo's large beach towel and climb onto its purplish-blue back, working frantically to revive him. Strange muted animal sounds emerge from inside the form as they lean into his back, pressing out lake water, which gushed at first from one side of his mouth.

"Dear God!" Joseph prays. "Please save him! Dear God, if you're a good God, a kind God, a God of mercy and miracles, please don't let this happen to Raymond! Please, dear God, can't You see? We're too young. He's just a young boy!"

For a few agonizing minutes, there is only Joseph on the lakefront watching the two older boys working feverishly to try to revive the limp, purplish-blue unrecognizable form that had to be Raymond. While the search was on, Shlomo and Danny have disappeared from fright; the little old lady probably dragged his younger brother home to avoid being drawn any further into the monstrous clutches of this local farm and lake tragedy. Joseph cannot think of leaving although a part of him desperately wants to run away and escape from the horror! He feels certain that reviving Raymond is an impossible task. Yet for some incomprehensible reason, Joseph is fixated on seeing the drowned boy's face; sooner or later, they'll have to turn him over and reveal his face. The nearly naked body in black swimming trunks with a muddied white stripe down its sides seems much too small to be Raymond, more like a second grader. *Stupid! Who else could it be?* What can his distressed mind be thinking? What kind of confirmation can he possibly be searching for in his craze to see the limp form's face close-up?

All at once, a miraculous transformation takes place at Philips Lake. The lakefront has become the center of a major rescue effort filled with loud, shattering noise and fierce energy from teams of firemen, policemen, neighborhood workers, and several different types of life-saving trucks and equipment. The two older boy rescuers are roughly shunted aside by a grown-up crew of emergency professionals and medical men, who know their jobs. They quickly sweep in to administer an injection and feed oxygen from a large tank to the limp purplish-blue form. But as only Joseph knows, Raymond must have been underwater caught in the weeds for almost half an hour. How can they possibly save him after all that time with so much water in his lungs and his brain dead from lack of oxygen? *Saving him is impossible! And it's all our fault. Why, in God's name, didn't I…Why didn't any of us notice that Raymond was missing?*

At YMCA camp, counselors set up a buddy system. Whenever they blew a whistle, the boys were expected to know exactly where your buddy was, find him, and raise your linked hands in the air. But we had no lifeguard or counselors and no buddy system, except for the natural one of Shlomo and Danny as brothers. Poor Raymond had no buddy. I should have been his buddy. Why didn't I think of that? If I cared for him at all and was his buddy, I would have immediately noticed he was missing, and we could have tried to save him a half hour earlier!

First thing, I would have sent Shlomo to the house by the road to call emergency. Then I'd swim out to the rowboat, grab the oars to help me float, and begin diving or feeling underwater with my arms and legs for any part of Raymond's body that was caught below in the weeds. With no lifeguard, I was the only one able to swim well enough to try to save him. "Why didn't he see Raymond's absence immediately as soon as he got Danny to shore? How could he not have noticed and at least tried to rescue him?" Guilt at his not missing Raymond at all and guilt about not trying to save him worked its insidious way into Joseph's conscience.

"Stop blaming yourself!" he can hear his mother's voice demanding. "You could have drowned too if you'd gone back and dived down into those treacherous weeds in search of Raymond's body. Then there might have been a double tragedy." *She's right, but I should have noticed and tried! Wasn't it a crime that I didn't even notice?*

But the war game itself was his fault, especially the stupid idea of taking that leaking rowboat out across the lake. All of his crazy war game ideas, as Shlomo called them, have come home to roost and led to an innocent boy drowning. *No question, Raymond will die. His living spirit must already be beyond saving, and I'll have to face up to that terrible reality for all of eternity!*

Dark thoughts keep crashing down into Joseph's mind at high speed. He vividly recalls the noise he heard behind him as he abandoned ship and dove excitedly toward shore. Could his excited, life-saving dive to shore, his own body's forward surge, have thrown Raymond off-balance, maybe smashing his head against the bow or the oarlocks and maybe knocking him totally unconscious? These black dog thoughts, which might be true, race across Joseph's mind at the speed of light. Wait! If his dive caused the boat to rock back and smash into poor Raymond's head, there would have to be bruises, cuts, or swelling on his head near his hairline that would be easy to see with his blond crewcut. Now Joseph has the most compelling reason in the world to try to see Raymond's face and head close-up, so he ducks underneath the lifeguard's chair and slides his body quietly along the sand, determined to get one close look at Raymond's face for evidence of his own innocence or proof of his absolute guilt.

The professional rescue team has Raymond's limp purplish-blue form laid out on a tarp next to the high lifeguard's chair. They are administering oxygen, shots of adrenaline, and what looks like a wand giving off a series of electrical jolts. The boy's form jumps up, levitates, then folds back onto the tarp. Joseph has snaked his body along the sand under the lifeguard's chair, unnoticed by the rescuers until his face is within a yard or two of Raymond's face, which is still hidden beneath the oxygen mask. Joseph lies there patiently with a single-minded focus. Sooner or later, he knows the rescuers will lift the mask, and for a brief second, Joseph will have his desperately needed close look. He must concentrate on seeing any sign of bruises, cuts, or swelling on Raymond's face or head. It is increasingly difficult to see anything now with the rescuers' heavy legs and large bodies constantly stomping about in front of the form, so Joseph slides himself even closer to the edge of the tarp to within a few feet of Raymond's face. He listens to the boy's artificial breathing sounds, a reminder of his earlier asthmatic groans. If they'll only remove the mask for one second!

Suddenly, Joseph feels two huge hands grip his short crewcut and pull his body out from under the lifeguard's chair, dragging him across the sand, yards away from the drowned boy's rescuers.

"Get out of our hair you crazy little bastard! What the hell are you, some kind of ghoul or kid creep?" For a split second, Joseph is afraid that those huge hands may belong to Raymond's father. Joseph is terrified to think what Raymond's policeman father might do to him once the policeman learns that Joseph's war game was the reason they took the rowboat out across the lake—and after it sank, him not even noticing that Raymond was missing. But luckily, a fireman's cap is attached to the huge angry man shaking him roughly by his hair and throwing him into the bushes.

Joseph instantly jumps to his feet and dodges back past the fireman, more desperate to get a close look at Raymond's head for any sign of cuts, swelling, or bruises. The huge fireman is furious; he catches Joseph again—this time by his ears—lifts the boy off his feet onto his shoulder, and dumps him right in the middle of the crowd of onlookers.

"Stay away, little Creep! Keep out of our way, or I'll have the Sheriff arrest you! We're trying to save a boy's life!"

Behind him, Joseph hears the muted voice of a neighborhood woman say, "He's one of them, one of them Jewish City kids who broke into the lake and stole the rowboat."

Joseph feels people's eyes turn on him, but he keeps his own focus on the rescuers working over Raymond's limp body, which is totally naked now, stripped of his bathing trunks as they cover his form with brown army blankets. Two policemen arrive on the scene. One who towers over all the other rescuers drops to his knees onto the tarp and places his arms around the boy, hugging him; then he begins adjusting the boy's oxygen tank. The powerful tall man must be Raymond's policeman father, although Raymond is pretty much of average size for a ten-year-old, not the giant of a son you might expect. "Out of the way, everyone! Move!" a fireman hollers as they back an ambulance to the edge of the tarp. It's hard to see exactly what is happening now, but they're placing Raymond's body on a stretcher, about to lift it into the back of the ambulance. Joseph breaks out of the crowd and edges close to the open truck door; he must see if Raymond is still breathing and whether there are cuts or bruises on his forehead.

As the door is about to close, a huge arm locks under his chin and lifts Joseph up and away from the stretcher and truck door. "Holy shit! You're not the same creepy kid!" the huge fireman announces. Now they've closed the rear door of the ambulance and are about to whisk Raymond's body off to the hospital emergency room. Inside is the towering policeman along with three medical-men rescuers. The ambulance pulls away very slowly at first without using its siren. It comes to a stop halfway up the dirt driveway, pausing for several minutes while the rescuers shift around inside, still working to save the boy's life; then it moves off quickly onto the main road, turning on its loud siren as it exits. How can it possibly be that Raymond is not already dead? Joseph wonders. Yet they're acting as if they can still save him. It was all too surreal and confusing. The huge fireman dumps Joseph roughly into the weeds, far away from the departing crowd. "Go home, little Creep! There's nothing left here for you to see!"

The little Creep lowers his head in shame, his body trembling badly as he makes his way through the dispersing crowd and noisy trucks out through the wide-open front gates without truly seeing or hearing anyone. Unconsciously, he turns left into a hilly road he's never taken before, and after a quarter mile or so, he stumbles off the macadam into the woods, finding himself in the midst of a thicket of very sharp prickers. Instead of trying to extricate himself stem by stem, the boy pushes stupidly ahead; all the scratches he feels as he passes through the thorny plants seem a just, deserving punishment for his sin of being the person most responsible for Raymond's tragic death. His bleeding from the thorns is just a start to his penitence. Joseph tries to accept pain from the cuts and scratches as well as pain from his hair where the huge fireman had lifted him and from the constant throbbing in his ankle from his jump off the bungalow roof that morning, which seems like an eternity ago.

Feelings of guilt nearly overwhelm all pain as he plunges into the shadows of the darkening afternoon forest, and he imagines he sees a naked, purplish-blue form disappear, like the Jackson-White boy, into a cluster of trees hundreds of yards ahead of him. He feels compelled to follow this unreal, ghoulish image along that same path step by step. The image disappears then emerges again, seated beside the hollow trunk of a tree broken in two by lightning. The image sits there motionless, its back to Joseph, as if in a trance of its own. Terrified but compelled to approach the image, Joseph moves close behind, about to tap its right shoulder.

The blurry image, sensing his presence, swivels its head backward in an uncanny angular rotation to face Joseph. It is the image of Raymond's swollen face, gulping and then gushing out lake water from one side of its mouth. And there on the left side of the image's head behind his left ear, Joseph sees what looks like a large swelling, a bad bruise. As he tries to get a sharper, more definitive look, the image suddenly vanishes, and he finds himself alone beside the hollow, fallen tree.

Joseph, who seeks out the solitude of forests, content listening to the sound of birds and other small creatures scurrying through the leaves, often stalking animals like a predator to perfect his hunting skills or hiding away for hours in his cave reading books about primitive people and the natural foods of the forest, finds himself trembling with uncontrollable fear. These woods where Raymond's image has led him seem different from all other forests he's ever seen, part of a terror-filled countryside that is alive with strange, screeching sounds from a nearly human group of crows or black birds circling above then landing one by one on a nearby limb to watch him, as if aware of his every move. Off in the distance, images of rescuers' faces radiate high across the treetops as intense sunlight once throbbed across the surface of the lake. He hears the old lady's muted voice. "He's one of them, one of them City Jew boys who broke in and stole the rowboat, who stood by too frightened to act and let our policeman's son drown." Helpless to confront reality and alter the tragedy, Joseph tries desperately to will it out of his mind, to act as if this entire afternoon was a horrible dream, like hiding from that malodorous monster Grendel in the cave beneath the sea. He prays that he will awaken to a sunny new morning and this nightmare, like all nightmares before, will spontaneously end as if Raymond's tragic drowning never really happened!

Anxious and off-balance, the boy sets his internal compass toward the northwest, hoping to find his way back to those safe, familiar woods behind his home. It was then that Joseph becomes conscious of someone or something stalking him. Yet whenever he whirls around, all he sees is the image of the drowned boy's face and limp form projected onto the distant branches of ancient, weirdly shaped, human-looking trees. Months of self-training in willpower and courage are completely undermined, sapping all strength from his body and confidence from his mind. Joseph feels powerless to stay ahead of the wild forces catching up to him from behind. He finally breaks down and gives in, dropping face downward onto the fern-cushioned earth, where he listens to echoes of his shrieking plea to God Almighty bouncing back and forth across the forest floor: "Please save him, dear God! If you're a good God, a God of mercy and miracles like your son Jesus, able to bring people back from the dead. Please, dear God, bring Raymond back to life. He's just a boy! Save him, dear God, and I'll believe in you forever. Let me be your Instrument, Lord, I swear—forever!" Joseph feels lost in a world where death has its way and he can no longer create his heroic make-believe dreams, create his own destiny, and expect his own winning outcomes to always come true. Before, he truly believed that God, a primal force or great white-bearded patriarch, was with him, watching out for him, and that he'd always walk on the good side of God's shadow. Now Joseph feels only emptiness instead. The skies remain deep blue, but the heavens seem empty of meaning, and the universe is endlessly accelerating, racing away from him, toward what? What else but its sure destruction.

The incredulous reality of Raymond's drowning has cleaved a sharp black dagger into the boy's chest, and it will not disappear but is part of him as Joseph half-walks, half-runs back into the familiar woods behind their little farm past his own hidden cave, past Grandfather's outhouses and the rows of chicken coops, and past gaptooth Thomas's empty shack with its large black-and-white poster of Christ on the wall, all the way back to the front door of his family's bungalow home with its odd-shaped, broken, metallic mezuzah. He feels like a stranger to it all, and he is surprised, very nearly shocked by his mother's instant recognition.

"What's wrong?" Mother asks the moment he steps through the front door. Joseph shakes his head, unable to speak the words. It is clear that the rabbi's sons or their parents hadn't thought to communicate with Joseph's mother. The farmhouse next door stands silent, all of its wartime blackout curtains drawn tightly shut.

"Did something happen at the lake?" He can only nod his head. "Did one of the rabbi's sons get hurt?"

"A b-boy drowned," Joseph stammers.

"Was it one of them?"

"No, another boy. Three of us were…in a r-r-rowboat together. It s-sank. The other boy…d-drowned!"

Joseph breaks down, unable to tell her anything more. Mother takes him into her strong arms and rocks him back and forth like she did when he was her little baby, but this time, black dog thoughts of the drowning and the dagger in his chest cannot be washed away by the warmth of her love or the magic of her Russian peasant's ability to comfort and heal. "All of our wounds heal in time," Mother whispers. "Listen to me! Believe me! Time will heal everything!"

3

"The Valley chief of police called." Mother sighs, hanging their black party-line telephone back on its hook. "An officer is on his way here to talk with you this morning."

A week and a half has passed since the drowning. Joseph hears only that the boy died on his way to the hospital. Stories of the drowning are featured on the front pages of the two local newspapers, but the names of the other boys in the rowboat, Joseph's and Danny's names, were withheld due to their ages. Raymond was buried in a small Presbyterian churchyard surprisingly close to the lake in which he drowned. The children in his church class held a memorial service for him. Mother relates these events to Joseph but does not show him the newspaper articles. All morning, Joseph walks back and forth through the bungalow looking out of the sunroom windows, anxious for the policeman's car to arrive, apprehension building to a frantic pressure point inside him. Beneath the sunroom windows, Joseph's army of painted steel toy soldiers are deployed, silently guarding the castle fortress he'd created out of large hardcover books, mostly his father's old set of black *Encyclopedia Britannica* and children's adventure stories, many by Robert Louis Stevenson.

Today of all days, Joseph wishes to be the Shadow to cloud men's minds and turn invisible, able to observe the police officer's arrival and departure without being seen or having to answer a question, not a word. Old gaptooth Thomas once told him, "Our world is filled with invisible dead spirits milling about in different dimensions because so few are worthy enough to get through that tiny hole in a needle that gets you up into Heaven. And only the worst evil souls, who can't be absolved of mortal sin, get shuttled down into the fires of Hell." Raymond's soul may be doomed to stay close-by anyway, to walk the earth forever due to the horrible nature of his death. Joseph wonders if Raymond's spirit has the power to teleport itself into their house to watch the policeman's interrogation. If so, will the drowned boy's spirit make some sign or sound or cause the walls to shake like a low-level earthquake if he thinks Joseph is telling a lie or shading the truth in a self-serving way? A shiver runs through Joseph as he imagines a possible encounter with the drowned boy's ghost out to avenge his death and seeking some kind of eternal retribution.

"Just tell the officer the whole truth," Father advised before leaving for his office.

But is the whole truth that simple? Will his version of the drowning be different from that of the rabbi's sons? He wishes he knew what they said when interrogated two days after the drowning, but the rabbi and his family left, packed up, and went back to the City with hardly a word, owing his grandfather nearly a full month's rent. After their interrogation by the local police, Grandfather said the rabbi was very worried about an anti-Semitic reaction since the three Jewish boys were the only ones involved in the drowning of a Christian boy—what's more, the son of a local officer of the law. The rabbi was furious with his sons and angry at Joseph for leading them into the illegal, closed lake and for involving Danny in his war game and "seducing" him onto the unsafe rowboat. He held no appreciative feeling toward Joseph for helping rescue his younger son by pushing him safely to shore. But if Shlomo hadn't hollered out "Help! You've got to save Danny!" Joseph is convinced he would have noticed that Raymond hadn't come up to the surface. He would have sent Shlomo for help while he swam out to the boat to try to rescue the boy. And surely, the older boys would have been alerted and arrived sooner; those extra ten or fifteen minutes could have saved Raymond's life. Joseph shudders when he thinks about the closeness of life and death.

What if Raymond's spirit is on its way here right now, sitting in the car alongside the policeman, and will be entering this room with him to witness the official police interview? What version of truth does the drowned boy believe? he wonders. What lies or omissions will he watch for? Or, God help us, is it possible his spirit will appear and point a finger at a lump or cut or bruise on his own ghostly head and reveal Joseph's guilt to all the world? When a spirit materializes, gaptooth Thomas insists, we must keep our guard up and expect the unexpected.

Why does the truth seem so incomplete and foggy? Joseph wonders, continuing to scratch the front of his crewcut. Why, even he can't swear to his own version of everything that might have happened. And what did the rabbi's sons tell the police? Did they place all the blame on him? "Joseph promised to take us swimming. The lake was closed, but Joseph broke open the gate and led us in. The others came later—Raymond and the older boys. But Joseph was the one who challenged the drowned boy and Danny to take that leaky rowboat out across the lake with his crazy war game," Shlomo will say. "I warned Danny not to go along with them. I tried to stop him, but he was drawn into the war game by Joseph's challenge, not wanting to be looked at as too soft or a baby." And after the rowboat sank, did Shlomo tell the police how Joseph swam over and helped save Danny's life? Probably he did; it would add sympathy for them and understanding. They hadn't noticed Raymond missing, Shlomo can say because "I was working on top of Danny, who'd swallowed all that lake water and was feeling sick and scared to death from his near drowning. But Joseph was just sitting on the beach with nothing to do. He's the one who should have remembered Raymond, shouldn't he?" Was that their version, or did they invent other incriminating actions that may or may not have happened? Theirs could be a far different story or a scared or confused one. Whatever, it could only be part of the truth. They sensed nothing of Joseph's own worrisome dive toward shore and its possible tragic implications.

Joseph was more anxious about Raymond's version if his spirit was hovering about. Raymond might say, "I was just passing by on the road when I saw the Jewish boys inside the lake swimming. I found the front gate halfway open, so I went in to join them." Raymond might throw in an unexpected idea like, "I found the rowboat and turned it over, but I was just going to paddle that old boat close along the shoreline, which would have been safe. It was Joseph who challenged us to take it across the lake. Joseph swam out to the raft, so shouldn't he have known about all those dangerous weeds hiding beneath the water's surface?" Then he might say something nasty like, "Those Jew kids stick together, they didn't give a damn about me, they never noticed that I was underwater drowning, and they didn't lift a hand to save me." Worst of all he might say, "When Joseph dove off to abandon ship, the rowboat surged backward with great force, driving me forward, and my head hit the rail on the bow of the boat. I must have fallen into the water unconscious. Didn't Joseph hear the blow he caused? Didn't he think to look back to see if I was all right?"

Yes, he'd be right. I'm almost sure I heard a crash as I dove. Why didn't I dive off more carefully or swim to the far side of the boat to make sure that

Raymond was safe and able to make it to shore? No, the truth is, I never thought of Raymond's welfare for a single moment, never thought of him as a buddy to take care of. All true, Joseph had to admit. He'd been lost in his own world playing his own stupid games; he was even excited by the act of abandoning ship. His self-image was that of Tarzan screaming out across the jungle as he dove into alligator-infested waters, if the truth be known. Dammit! Was there a cut or bruise on the dead boy's head or not? he wonders. If only the rescuers had taken the oxygen mask off the dying boy's face for just a second. How unreal and foggy the whole truth can be, and it all depends on your perspective. *Yes, everyone's truth will be different depending on which of the boys you happened to be. What is the whole truth, Father? Why is it so complicated?*

Whatever the story, none of us can change the outcome: a young boy drowned, and all that he was or ever would be has disappeared from the face of the earth. The stark image of Raymond's desk left empty in his classroom when school starts this fall breaks Joseph up and haunts him. He cannot fight off the tightness in his chest or stop the flow of tears each time he pictures Raymond's young classmates staring at his empty desk as they tiptoe by on the way to their seats. *Their teacher arrives and calls the roll. There is a moment of silence after which the children recite the Lord's Prayer. "Our Father, who art in Heaven..." A still moment to stop and consider how fragile human life can be.*

Yet, Joseph reminds himself, the whole world is at war. Thousands of soldiers and civilians are dying on five continents each and every day, so why let the death of one boy overwhelm him? He must learn to harden himself against this death and all future deaths, even the death of his own family and all his loved ones. Sooner or later, everyone on this earth dies. "Except Jesus Christ," old Thomas says, "who came back to life. Believe it!" The boy desperately wants to believe in an afterlife for

Raymond in Heaven with the fervor of gaptooth Thomas. Wonderful to believe that God looked down kindly on Raymond and that he is up there now in God's loving hands. But Joseph can't seem to hold that benevolent afterlife image in his head; instead, he keeps picturing the stark reality of Raymond's school desk left empty and the frightened looks on the faces of all his young classmates as they tiptoe by his unseen form. The raw emotion of that vivid scene seizes and overwhelms Joseph; he cannot focus on any other reality. Images of Raymond in Heaven blow away in the wind.

Outside, watching through the sunroom windows, Joseph's eyes catch the streaky motion of a black police car as it swerves off the road into their driveway, racing past the main farmhouse, and braking to a screechy halt on the lawn beneath his favorite cherry tree. Despite its speedy arrival, the police officer doesn't leave the car at once; he sits there motionless, as if deep in thought and fighting through his own emotions. Joseph feels a rush of sweat running down his face. It is another bright, hot, sunny day, a continuation of the two-week heat wave.

"The police officer is here now," Mother says quietly, looking out the living room window. "Are you ready to speak with him?"

The tightness in Joseph's chest returns, and he cannot answer her. After a few more minutes in solitary thought, the policeman finally opens the patrol car door and rises to his full height. He is a tall, broad-shouldered giant, who strides around the patrol car with forceful deliberation. As Joseph feared and expected, he's the same tall policeman who'd gotten into the back of the rescue truck along with the purplish-blue, blanketed body of his naked son, Raymond. Upon seeing him stride toward their front door, Joseph begins to tremble, and chills run down the back of his neck. He cannot stop his hands from shaking and crams them into his pants' pockets to hide them. *How can I face this intense policeman, this angry, disturbed father whose son I helped drown, the son whose young body lies in a grave and who no longer exists on this earth?* Joseph desperately wants to run off, to disappear, but he feels cornered in the sunroom of his own home, surrounded by his small army of steel toy soldiers, and there is nowhere else to run and hide.

Mother is speaking with the officer by the front door. She hopes that he remembers her playing on the women's high school championship basketball team with his older sister, the team's star player. She tells him how sorry they all are about the tragic loss of his only son, and her voice sounds just right, filled with true compassion. Then she leads him into the sunroom, where Joseph is waiting, hands in his pants' pockets.

"Joseph, this is Raymond Senior, the boy's father. He needs to ask you some questions," Mother says then exits from the room and takes the baby outside so there'd be no disturbance.

The tall policeman nods; he stands erect by the window, watching Mother go outdoors with the baby in her arms. Finally, he turns to face Joseph, who is seated on the window bench, his hands badly shaking. Raymond's father takes off his dark-blue aviator sunglasses and stares down into Joseph's eyes, taking the measure of this young boy, who was the last person his son saw before he drowned. The intensity of the officer's look is blinding, causing the boy to lower his head in shame. Confrontation with this giant policeman seems unreal to Joseph, like facing a sheriff from the cinema with his high cheekbones, tight lips, and square jaw, a man used to giving orders to outlaws and killers rather than asking questions of a frightened young boy. It is still difficult for Joseph to believe that this larger-than-life policeman with high black leather boots can be poor little Raymond's biological father. Then Joseph catches a quick glimpse of nearly dried tears that have run down the sides of the police officer's face; embarrassed, the boy lowers his head again and has to look away.

"Tell me what happened at the lake, son." "Yessir," Joseph says, trying to clear the phlegm from his throat. He starts by telling the police officer about the rabbi's sons cornering him while up in the cherry tree, begging him to take them swimming, and then getting his mother's permission. How, after the boys walked all that way, the rabbi's sons were disgusted to find Philips Lake closed.

"Did you see the sign on the gate?" "Yessir." "Did you read it?" "Yessir." "Do you know what 'Closed, absolutely no admittance' means?" "Yessir." "Yet you broke in. You decided you people were above the law?"

"It was a very hot d-day, Sir, hotter than today. We'd walked over three miles through the woods. We had no idea it w-wouldn't be open."

"You decided walking there gave you the right to break in?"

It would have been better to say nothing more, to not try to defend himself, but Joseph feels compelled to speak and try to explain. For young Raymond's sake, if his ghostly spirit is present, as well as his father's. So he closes his eyes and begins to speak.

"One side of the g-gate was hanging part open, Sir. And we thought we heard v-voices…older boy's voices inside." Well, he told his first lie. Will the policeman be able to read his face, he wonders, and know he is lying?

"The owner of Philips Lake swore in his affidavit that the gate was kept well locked. Is he telling the truth?"

"Maybe he thought it was locked, Sir." The officer pauses for a long moment, studying Joseph's face; he'd been caught in a lie with the very first question.The boy feels angry at himself. He must stick to the truth from here on out, even if the truth works against him.

"One of the witnesses we spoke with, I won't name him, said you were the boy who broke open the gate."

"Yessir, I p-pushed my shoulder against it, and the lock pretty much fell away on its own. That's the t-truth, Sir." Or close enough, Joseph hopes.

"And you couldn't have heard the voices of older boys inside since they arrived well after you and the Issenberg brothers."

"Yessir, that's true." The policeman's intense face has turned very unsympathetic, openly revealing his disappointment with Joseph.

"From this point forward, I do not want to hear another lie! Is that clear?" The tall policeman's eyes flash out in anger.

"Yessir. C-clear, Sir."

"You broke the law by unlawful entry. You led the other boys inside the well-posted lake property. If you hadn't broken in, none of this would have happened. My son would not have gone into Philips Lake to join you. My son would be alive today!"

"Yessir." Oh my God! Raymond's father blames him for losing his son. That is clear already. The officer truly hates him for breaking the law and opening the gate. Like opening Pandora's box, his was the original sin. Joseph trembles, now wondering if it is in this giant police officer's power to recommend sending him to reform school for the act of illegal trespassing leading to an unlawful death. Could it turn out that badly?

"I'm sorry for what I d-did, Sir," Joseph blurts out. "I d-didn't mean to do any harm to R-Raymond or to anyone else."

"Yet you broke in. You felt you were above the law!"

Joseph remembers thinking how his Bubby Sarah would have been proud of his initiative in breaking in, how she, like most poor people—Jews and other immigrants—had a hatred of gates built to keep them out. Well, Raymond's father is right. He did feel pride at breaking in at first. Yet he must try to explain his act to make it seem less unlawful. It's not like they broke into a jewelry store or into a neighbor's home to steal money or their tools. Or even like the pickers who stole Grandfather's chickens.

"We thought we could take a quick d-dip and leave. The rabbi's sons were awful tired and all sweaty from the hot sun, and we had a long walk b-back home ahead of us without getting to go in the water."

The policeman's voice lowers and grates with anger. "There is no excuse for breaking the law! Absolutely no excuse!" His eyes glare out at the boy from beneath his bushy light eyebrows.

"Yessir. I can see you're right, Sir. I was just t-trying to explain why w-we—" Joseph stops, realizing that any further attempt to explain is making things worse with Raymond's father. He must stop trying to explain, just accept his guilt, and take whatever punishment the law decides. But it may be hard on him, maybe even unfair.

"You swam out to the raft, they said, when you first got there?"

"I d-did, Sir. The rabbi's sons stayed near the shore, splashing water on each other. Then they started making castles in the sand."

"Do you consider yourself a good swimmer?"

"Yessir, I guess so. My mother taught me how to swim when I was little. The b-back stroke, the b-breast stroke, the Australian crawl—"

"Continue! What happened? What happened next?" he orders in a gruff voice, almost a growl, and Joseph wonders what it was he said that brought on the policeman's sudden ferocity again.

"I swam back from the raft, and I climbed up onto the lifeguard's chair to see if anyone was w-watching us from the road. That's when I saw…when I first saw R-Raymond looking at us from outside the south f-fence. I guess he was just w-walking down the road and saw us inside the lake. Is that right, Sir? Or was he c-coming here to swim?"

Raymond's father is strangely silent. "Whatever we did, Raymond saw the No Admittance sign too. So if we broke the law, he did too" Joseph wants to add, but he is afraid to say it aloud to the police officer.

"Next time I saw him, he was inside the lake—right next to us along the shore, doing his exercises on the lifeguard's chair."

"Exercises?" the policeman asked, scratching his eyebrow.

"He did a whole lot of chin-ups, push-ups…hanging by his legs…sh-showing off his m-muscles. Then he found the old rowboat stuck in the weeds and turned it right-side up. That's when he na-knocked Danny and Shlomo's clothes, which were on the rowboat, all over the ground."

"The Issenberg boys didn't mention anything to us about their clothes being thrown to the ground."

"They wouldn't, Sir. Your son…I think he kind of s-scared them."

"Hard to believe that," the policeman said, shaking his head again.

"It's the t-truth, Sir, I swear. After Raymond t-turned the rowboat over, he got inside and started cleaning all the mud off the oars. Raymond was acting like the boat b-belonged to him."

"You're saying it was Raymond who found the rowboat?"

"Yessir. Then he asked me to help him drag it into the water."

"One of the witnesses said you were the one who called for help."

"I d-did, Sir, when Raymond and I were having a hard time g-getting it across a c-crevice between the g-grass and sand."

"So you could start to play your idiotic war game?"

"Nossir, so Raymond could get his r-rowboat into the water. He loved boats, he said. He told me all about how you and his uncle, the Marine, used to t-take him d-deep-sea fishing in the Sound and in the Atlantic Ocean before the war."

"My son told you that?" he asked, scratching his eyebrow again.

"Yessir. Isn't that the truth, Sir?"

The policeman coughed. Then in a gruff, reflective tone said, "Once. We took Raymond with us once when he was small. He got seasick and threw up. My brother and I seldom went deep-sea fishing, and we never took Raymond again. It's hard for me to believe he told you that he loved boats."

"He d-did, Sir. I swear to you he said that."

The tall policeman rose and covered his eyes with his dark sunglasses once more, and he stared past the painted steel toy soldiers and out the sunroom window for several minutes, acting as if Joseph was no longer there.

So Raymond made it up about always going deep-sea fishing with his father and uncle, the Marine, and loving boats so much. Well, maybe that's what he really wanted to do and couldn't, but why lie about it to me? Was it part of his act to try to live up to his father's policeman image and scare other kids off so they wouldn't challenge him? Was he vulnerable in some way and hiding it? Joseph remembers feeling that Raymond was the real thing, brought up in a family of hard men—hunters, riflemen, deep-sea fishermen, and genuine war heroes—while the rabbi's sons were soft City Jews, and Joseph himself was somewhere in the middle, mostly living in his world of make-believe but confident that he was training to be a brave soldier too. Yes, he'd be one of them someday.

"He was real proud of you, Sir, being a policeman and knowing all about g-guns and boats, and fishing. And p-proud of his uncle too."

"My brother? What did he tell you about my brother?"

"A lot, Sir. That he's a Leatherneck, a Marine who's f-fighting the Japs on Guadalcanal or some island in the Pacific Ocean. That you really want to be over there fighting alongside your brother, Sir, but they need you here for security at home, and they w-won't let you enlist in the Marines." Once more, Raymond's father stares out the sunroom window, reflecting. Was it true about his father and uncle? Joseph starts to wonder whether Raymond had made up some or even most of it. His father says nothing, so it might all be true. Or not...

"You and Raymond dragged the rowboat into the lake. What happened next?" This part is frightening to Joseph and brought on deep emotions of regret and guilt. "Go ahead. Tell me what happened next?"

For the first time in his life, Joseph begins to stutter so badly that he cannot get the words out. Oh, he'd stumbled over some words before, increasingly so since the drowning, but never as badly as this. The tall policeman lets him flounder for a few seconds but becomes impatient.

"That's when you challenged the boys to your war game, a game that involved a dangerous, irresponsible mission—trying to paddle that leaking, unsound rowboat clear across the lake. Correct?"

"Yessir," he says, relieved that the officer was so provoked that he said it for Joseph, who added "We were g-going to s-surprise the Nazi and Italian g-guards hiding in the trees on the other shore."

"Why did you want to challenge the boys to a war game?"

"I just th-thought it would be f-f-f—exciting, Sir." The policeman stares down at the placement of the boy's platoon of colorful steel toy soldiers guarding the windowsill fortress. He shakes his head, about to react, but manages to hold back his emotions.

"All Joseph cares about is playing war games, the Issenberg boys told us. It's his favorite thing to do. So you find war fun and exciting. You like to compete and beat other boys like Raymond? You like to play at war and win, do you?"

"As a t-team, Sir. I wanted to t-team up with Raymond and see if we two could win a tough b-b-battle together. It's like b-boot camp training, Sir. All of us kids started doing it right after P-Pearl Harbor when w-war was d-declared, and we were scared the Nazis m-might invade America. All of us p-play war games, Sir. We keep t-testing and t-training ourselves every day." He wanted to ask "Didn't Raymond?" But he held back.

"So you were showing off to the other boys, you wanted to test them, and you picked the stupidest, most dangerous target out of thin air for all of you—to try to cross the lake in that hopelessly leaking rowboat?"

"I d-don't know, Sir. You c-c-could be right."

The officer was right about showing off, but it wasn't for the rabbi's sons; they were soft and didn't even like the idea of playing war games. It was mostly for Raymond's benefit and his own, Joseph had to admit. It was his chance to take command of the rowboat and challenge the boy, to see if he could keep up with Raymond physically, outlast him, or get the better of him in the game, using his own cunning and willpower, to act like the natural leader he wanted to be and to take charge, if he could manage it. That was the truth, but he could never dare admit that truth to Raymond's father, who was glaring out at him again.

"You're a good swimmer. You had no doubt you'd be able to make it back to shore if the rowboat went under, which even a class idiot could see was the most likely outcome."

What is he getting at? Joseph wonders. Is it that Danny couldn't swim well? That I forced him or teased him into coming along with us?

"I d-didn't want D-Danny along, Sir. I d-didn't think he was a g-good enough swimmer. He had to show us—Raymond and me—that he could d-dog-paddle good enough to stay afloat."

"Raymond and you tested him?"

"We did, Sir." The policeman shakes his head sadly; he takes off his dark sunglasses again and wipes at the dried-up tears on one side of his face with the dark-blue sleeve of the police shirt. *What's wrong?* Joseph wonders. *What am I missing?* All of a sudden it dawns on Joseph that he never actually saw Raymond swim; he never saw him drown, but he never saw him swim. He did see him wash himself down with lake water at first with all that asthmatic breathing, but not dive or swim in it. *No, it's not possible, is it?* Joseph finds himself making a dumb statement instead of asking the question he really wants to ask.

"R-Raymond kind of said he was a pretty g-g-good swimmer, Sir."

"Raymond told you that?" The policeman is angry again and shaking his head. Joseph is frightened now. There was no way he should have told a direct lie to the boy's father.

"N-Not exactly said that, Sir. B-But with his love of b-b-boats and deep-sea fishing and you being a p-police officer and your family all being athletes, fishermen, and M-Marines—" Joseph stops. My God, is it possible that he never saw the drowned boy actually swim and just assumed that he swam well?

Joseph is now desperate to ask the tight-lipped officer, "Is it possible, Sir, that you never taught your son, Raymond, how to swim? Was there something wrong with him, like that heavy breathing? Or was there a problem between you and him? Wasn't he a good enough son, or maybe you weren't around enough to bother to teach him?" These questions hung in the air between them, but Joseph can't bring himself to ask them directly. Instead, he asks.

"W-Why would R-Raymond have g-gone out with us across the lake in the first p-place, Sir, if he w-w-wasn't a really good swimmer?" Was he afraid to back off from Joseph's challenge, or could there be something deeper? Could the boy have been slow or kind of retarded, or is it possible that he had some other hard-to-notice physical or mental disability?

All of these disturbing, unanswered questions wash over Joseph's mind, but he gets no answers from the policeman, only an odd kind of silence. If Raymond couldn't swim well—and Joseph never did ask him—trying to cross the lake in a leaky rowboat was an insane act, like diving off a cliff without a glider or parachute. Maybe there was a mental problem he had to deal with, but there's no chance that his father will tell him about it now. Raymond's policeman father and Joseph sit together on the bench of the sunroom for a long while, each deep in their own thoughts, saying nothing to each other.

Mother comes to the door, drawn there by the silence, but seeing them together and Joseph safe, she disappears back into the kitchen without comment.

"How is it possible that none of you boys noticed that Raymond was missing? That he was underwater and drowning when the rowboat sank?" the police officer demands in a gruff, precise way, as if he is talking about someone other than his own dead son.

"I d-don't know, Sir! I yelled 'Abandon ship,' and d-dove toward shore, but I w-went down too d-deep, and my arms and legs got all caught up in the w-weeds. When I f-fought my way to the surface, the first thing I heard was Shlomo hollering, 'Help! Danny can't make it to shore!' So I s-swam over, got behind him and p-pushed D-Danny in close enough to shore where he c-could stand. Then I walked him in, and Shlomo began to w-work on top of him, yelling and c-cursing until Danny sat up on his own. After that, we b-both looked b-back at the lake…saw the sunken b-boat and two oars and we b-both thought of R-Raymond. Just then, the three older b-boys came running back down b-because of all Shlomo's yelling, and Shlomo t-told them straight out that R-Raymond was—missing!"

"The boys said you ran off somewhere and didn't help them try to rescue my son?" he said quietly, staring intensely at Joseph.

"Not true, Sir. I t-tried h-hard to find him. I ran all over. First, I thought he m-might be hiding behind the r-raft. Then I went up the driveway to look in the ch-changing rooms. I was s-sure he'd made it safe out of the water and was hiding somewhere, just t-trying to f-fool us. I swear, Sir, I just c-couldn't b-believe it could be anything else!"

All at once, Joseph breaks down and begins to sob, his shoulders and back heaving. The tall policeman watches him break down but makes no attempt to step forward and comfort the boy. When Joseph finally gets control of himself, he senses that the interrogation is over. He desperately wants to ask the officer whether the police found any bruises or cuts on Raymond's head or evidence he might have been knocked unconscious when Joseph, overexcited and thinking only of himself, dove for shore. But he never gets to ask that question. The interview is clearly over, yet Joseph wishes that Raymond's father will say or do something personal or with kindness before he leaves. He doesn't expect words. He imagines the tall, gaunt man reaching out a hand, like a great black bear might extend a paw, to simply touch him or rest a huge paw on his shoulder. That might have been enough to help free Joseph of some of his guilt for a lifetime, but that too was not to be.

Instead, Raymond's father turns abruptly and leaves the sunroom hunched over slightly, not at his full height, as if suffering from a stitch in his stomach. Joseph watches through the sunroom window as Raymond's policeman father strides across the lawn to his patrol car; he slams the door loudly and guns the powerful engine, swinging the car out onto the macadam road with a screech of tires. If another auto had been on the road, he might have smashed head-on into it. The sound of his car's high- powered engine roars down the mountain road and disappears.

Mother enters, comforting the baby, who has begun to cry. She tries to read Joseph's face, "He didn't even say good-bye!" Joseph nods. She takes it to mean he'd survived.

Joseph sits quietly on the sunroom bench alongside his army of motionless toy soldiers and looks out at the cloudless afternoon sky. He wonders if the spirit of the dead boy had been in the room with them beside his father. No, not likely. There was something not right, out of balance between them. He wonders why Raymond's father did not act more proud or protective of his son. "We took him deep-sea fishing once, and never tried again." Joseph feels an overwhelming sense of sadness and sympathy for the drowned boy. Why didn't Raymond tell us that he wasn't a good swimmer? Why did he call the rowboat his and boss us around in order to get "his boat" into the water? Craziness!

Joseph sees the image of Raymond's empty desk in his classroom when school returns this fall, and the girls and boys tiptoe by, glancing at its emptiness on the way to their seats, showing greater respect for the boy in death than in life, with a sense of reverence or awe for his spirit. Their teacher calls the roll but stops when she comes to Raymond's name, and she skips over it. A long moment of silence, after which the children recite the Lord's Prayer. "Forgive us our trespasses and deliver us from evil…" Once again, the raw emotion of that vivid classroom image seizes and overcomes him; he cannot stop the tears from flowing down his face.

"God will forgive us our sins," Grandfather explains to Joseph on High holy day, "but not our sins against other people. Only they can forgive us for those sins." *Well, Raymond is gone and cannot forgive me if he wanted to. And Raymond's father could not forgive me even when I broke down, stammering, "I'm sorry, Sir. I swear." The tall policeman was incapable of even reaching out and touching my shoulder before driving off like a ferocious madman who couldn't get out of our house soon enough!*

Joseph feels left to hang in midair in a confusing kind of Purgatory space located somewhere between gaptooth Thomas's notion of Heaven and Hell. Hard men of war, like Raymond's father, seem incapable of forgiveness. Only softer, gentler men, non-warriors, like his grandfather or gaptooth Thomas seem truly capable of these acts, and they understand how badly a boy may need it.

That fall, Joseph spends early evenings sitting on the kitchen floor of the main farmhouse next to his grandfather, listening to war reports on the radio by the deep, comforting voice of Gabriel Heatter, who insists "There's good news tonight." Hitler, his Nazis, and the Japs are on the road to defeat; the world will return from the horror of never-ending death, mass killing, and slaughter of innocents and live in an era of peace that might be sustained for many generations. Over the next two years, they will learn about the Holocaust and of the development of an atomic bomb that wipes out cities, killing a hundred thousand human souls, and that has potential to destroy the entire planet if possessed by a race of crazy, uncompromising leaders, madmen like Hitler, bent on conquest or death and willing to bring the whole damned world down into the fires of Hell with them.

Joseph and his grandfather listen intently to the evening news as the warm, upbeat baritone voice soars across the continent and is magically captured, caught up like a thrown ball in space by a genie embedded in a crystal set properly tuned to a station number with its assigned frequencies. There is indeed good news tonight. The old man rubs the boy's hair as they listen together. "Once triumphant, we will never go to war again. This time the world will be much wiser. We will find a way," Grandfather promises. Joseph usually trusts the old man's optimism, but he's sensed how easily any of us can be drawn down dark pathways toward conflict and how fragile the unknown consequences are as we once again approach the locked garden gates. But there is nothing better than to sit there and dream with Grandfather in his warm kitchen.

Someday we may all live forever, and boys like Raymond will never drown!

———

Time Chords

The aftereffects of Raymond's drowning are profound for Joseph. He encounters a tightness inside his chest and stomach whenever made to speak in public, which first occurred when confronted by Raymond's father. Perhaps he stammered a bit before, but he begins to stutter so badly that he can no longer answer teachers' direct questions or spell words in class spelling bees or even say his own name or destination when getting on a bus. Words, especially consonants, don't come out easily. It got so bad that the following summer his parents sent him off to a speech clinic in the City, where mostly boys lie down to nap on mats after lunch, shut their eyes and listen to soft classical musical records and are asked to repeat the word, tranquility *in unison. They learn to wait patiently in class for what seems forever as each student stands and states his name, address, city, and state—and sometimes age. Joseph's stammer disappears only when singing songs, as well-crafted rhythmic lyrics float out like easy-flowing branches of a river in harmony, or when reading aloud to himself in the privacy of his own bedroom. His battle to overcome stuttering will plague him for most of his adult life.*

At night, Joseph comes to fear smothering in his sleep, an act not unlike drowning. While in REM sleep, he half-awakens to find himself facedown, nose and mouth jammed into a pillow or sheet cutting off his breath. He panics for there seems no communication between brain stem and cerebellum; he is unable to lift his head or shift his nose or mouth and open his respiratory system to oxygen-rich air or rid his lungs of carbon dioxide gas. He wants to scream out to his sleeping self, "Please, God! Lift your head. Turn your face so you can breathe!" At the last possible second before suffocating, it takes a Herculean effort involving all of his will to live to fight off that subterranean paralysis and lift his head aside. Fully awake, he lies there gasping for breath, frightened by this demonic inability to control these middle-of-night attacks, which occur several times a month. He tells no one about his seizures, certain that they are linked to the trauma of Raymond's drowning. Whether driven by guilt or a devilish curse from the dead boy or his policeman father, he feels as if mortal enemies have joined forces with an ancient angry god to punish him! "See what you did to me? This is what it's like to suffocate and drown!" He sleeps on his back, tosses his pillows onto the floor, and prays that these involuntary smothering attacks will pass over his house one night more. Mother told him about SIDS babies dying in their cribs, and he wonders if they too feel that subterranean tightening of the chest, paralysis, and loss of motor control and are simply too weak to lift their tiny heads from seizure, so they quietly pass away. Joseph's attacks of nighttime near-suffocation plague him for the next six or seven years. Then these traumas end, thank God, as suddenly as they began.

Ten years later, almost to a day in summer, the boy who lived on and did not drown meets a very pretty dark-haired young girl, instantly his soul mate, who by chance lived up the street from the boy who drowned, and she remembers how deeply that first tragic death had horrified all the seven-year-olds in her Bible class. She remembers Raymond wearing a brand-new gray suit to church the week before and how horrified they all were a week later to bury him in that same new gray suit. And now she too is dead before her time.

Strings of time vibrate, finger positions tremble, chords subtly change harmony and tempo as they surround and lock passing souls inextricably in certain places and times that once existed and now refuse to depart. Wise men claim that eleven or more dimensions exist, mathematical concepts immaculately designed to hint at the possibility of new pathways in and out of time, space, energy, and matter. And who of us is wise enough to say there are no second chances, that our endings may not be end-alls but vibrate into new beginnings? In Raymond's new beginning, he walks up to a fence with barbed wire atop, looks in, and sees no one about, sees only the glancing rays of sunlight bouncing off surfaces of lake water that will never have their chance to ambush him, surge into his lungs, and drown him. In that new beginning, Joseph and the rabbi's two sons return to the farm disappointed and frustrated, barely speaking for days. Raymond lives on in his second beginning to emulate his granite-faced father. He becomes a steadying point, a comfort to many, for in our new beginnings exists unnoticed wisdom absent in our first becoming. In the parallel universes that envelop us, the once dead retrace their steps, find new pathways, and prove far wiser about the hidden traps of time. They prize each moment of new beginnings in an intense and special way for they too can only guess whether this second chance is their final chance. Our wisest men ponder over eleven dimensions, and of the eleven, is there one dimension of space and time in which battered souls may linger, invisibly bound together in harmonic vibrations of love, peace, and yes, tranquility?

Cold-blooded realists will conclude that the drowning of a lone ten-year-old boy on a hot summer afternoon has little or no cosmic meaning beyond that of the accidental squashing of an ant beneath the grisly sole of a workman's leather boot, except to a few good souls clustered about him who loved or would have loved him given time. We feel mutations within mutations, moments in time when the strings pull tight, vibrate, and knots untie. Memories flow out and ripple in unending concentric circles that far outrun us in our lifetimes. A young girl child dies in a pandemic flu, devastating his grandfather's life and leaving the runt of the litter even more runt-like but a better man, perhaps, cut down to that smaller size and humbled.

If death has no dominion, our memories of an evitable drowning will live on with us in a multiverse of new beginnings. We may be free at last to alter life's frequencies, harmonics, and vibrations and perhaps unbind our spirits from the unjust knots of death itself.

We will come to live in a place where no one drowns the same way twice. Time chords? We may live to tell it.

The End

Made in the USA
Lexington, KY
13 March 2013